FISHING GUIDE TO

GEELONG — CORIO BAY
& THE BELLARINE PENINSULA

GEOFF WILSON

ACKNOWLEDGEMENTS

I gratefully acknowledge the following people for their help in gathering information on various aspects of fishing specifically in the task of putting together this most recent edition of **Fishing Geelong and the Bellarine Peninsula:**

Bob Grant for his knowledge of Queenscliff and Port Phillip Heads.

Arie De Wit for his freshwater input and photo opportunities.

Robert Coon for his companionship on many a fishing and exploratory trip to verify and update information.

Neil Walker President of Coastwatch Marine Rescue Ocean Grove for his information on boating and navigation.

Jeff Richards for his detailed knowledge of the Bellarine Peninsula and the fishing opportunities there.

Bill Athanasslies for the many photo opportunities he's provided me on a variety of fish from kingfish to large sharks from the Point Lonsdale pier.

I also acknowledge the large number of anglers who have provided me with fishing reports and photo opportunities for my weekly fishing column in the Geelong Advertiser which is now in its thirty second year. The most prolific of these include:

Brad Andrews, Steve O'Keefe, Justin Burns, Danny Skene, Keith Fry, Simon Werner, Daniel Stranger, Andrew Phillips, Rod Ludlow, Murray Scott, Scott Teasdale, Jeremy Barnes, Alex Andjelkovic and of course there are many others.

DISCLAIMER

Information published in this book should be used as a guide only. Maps should not be used for navigational purposes. Water depths shown on maps have been thoroughly reviewed at the time of publication but cannot be guaranteed. The changing nature of the marine environment suggests that some structures are likely to change in response to the forces of nature. Mariners should use the latest information available to plan safe passage through the waters described in this book.

First published 2012

Published and distributed by
Australian Fishing Network
PO Box 544 Croydon, Victoria 3136
Telephone: (03) 9729 8788 Facsimile: (03) 9729 7833
Email: sales@afn.com.au
Website: www.afn.com.au

©Australian Fishing Network 2012

ISBN: 9781 8651 3211 2

CONTENTS

INTRODUCTION

Fishing Geelong and the Bellarine Peninsula was first published in 1982 and has been revised several times since, this being the most recent.

The purpose of this publication has been to show the fishing potential in both salt and freshwater around the city of Geelong and as a reference for folk who want to take advantage of that potential.

The majority of folk who go fishing do so as an enjoyable recreation and this publication offers a number of options. For others fishing is a more serious affair that involves the specialized targeting of certain species, like large snapper that are not normally caught by the weekend punter.

Anglers have lost a good deal of access since when I was a youngster and was able to fish from almost all of the piers in Geelong, because – for one reason or another – anglers and other members of the public have been banned. Most of these restrictions have been imposed since this book's first publication in 1982.

Despite the fact that we recreational fishermen take few fish compared with our commercial counterparts, and generate substantially greater wealth for the community at large than does league football, the infra structure, such as boat ramps, provided for recreational fishermen is poor to say the least.

We have also been forced to accept the rampant ideology of marine parks where we cannot fish, reinforced by mumbo jumbo of the fascist greens that seems to be swallowed hook, line and sinker, not only by gullible members of the public but politicians and fisheries managers alike.

The good news is that we can still go fishing, but plotting the restrictions placed on us in recent years, on a graph, it would be fair to assume that in the not so distant future, recreational fishing with be restricted to designated puddles stocked with hatchery bred species any anglers worthy of the name would not bother with.

So, for the time being at least, let's enjoy fishing while we can, both to stock the larder and to enjoy and learn about marine and freshwater environments in a meaningful and practical way and hope that the future of this great activity is not as bleak as I suspect.

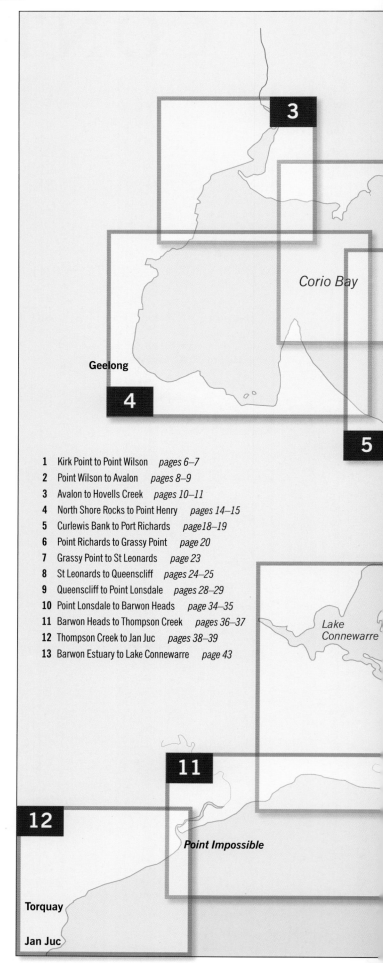

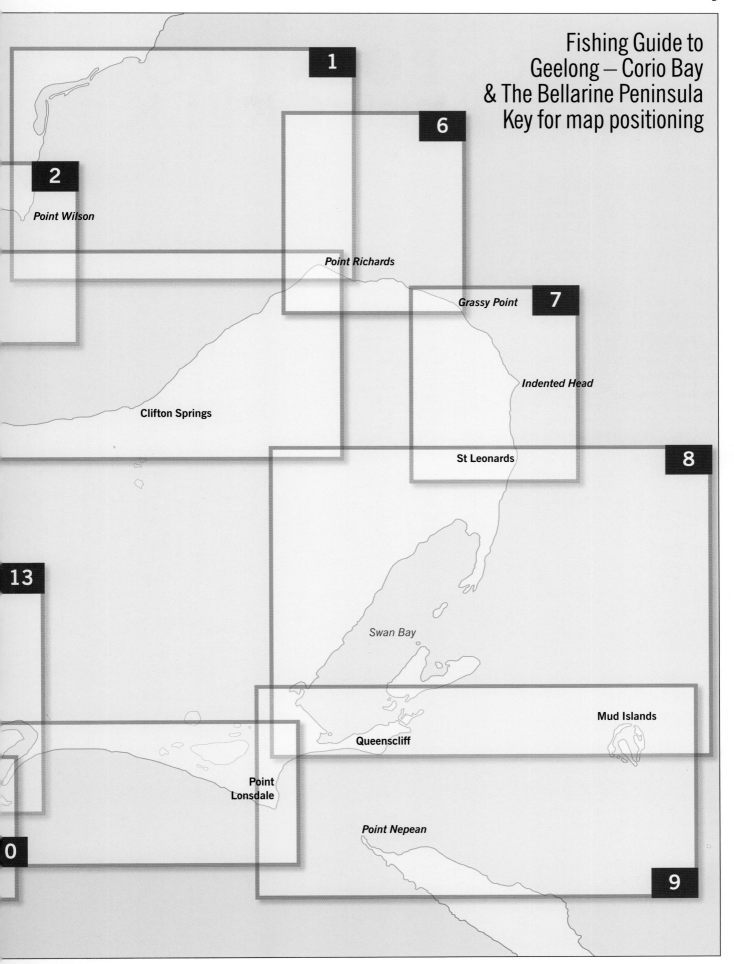

CHAPTER 1
KIRK POINT TO HOVELLS CREEK

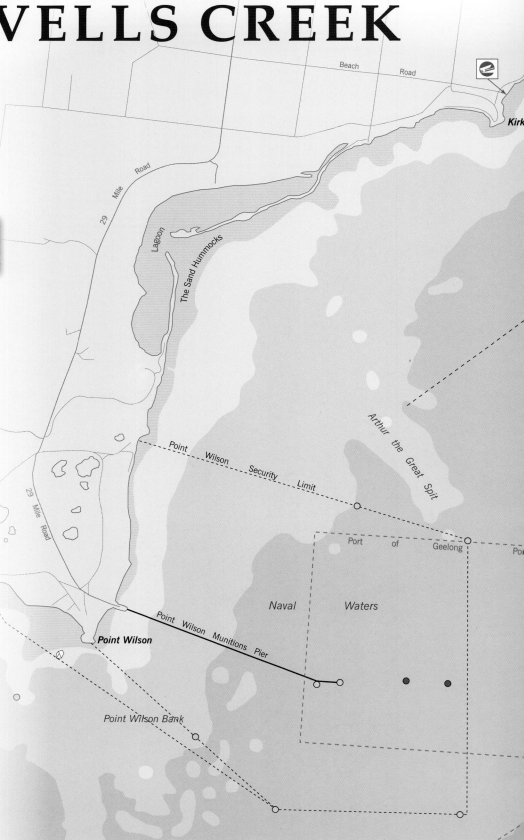

CORIO BAY

Corio Bay is divided into the inner and outer harbours by a sandbar which runs almost completely across the bay from Point Henry on the southern shore to Point Lillias to the north. Most fishing is by boat, but there are jetties and some other land based places to fish as well.

KIRK POINT TO POINT WILSON

KIRK POINT

There is a small boat ramp at Kirk Point that will accommodate craft to 5 m or so in good weather and favourable tidal conditions but it is exposed to weather from the east or south east, parking is limited, and there are some rock hazards at low tide. Access to Kirk Point is from the Avalon Airport exit (Beach Road) from the Princes Highway (Melway 424 F3).

LONG REEF

The feature known as Long Reef begins to the left (north) of the boat ramp and extends a kilometre or so seaward. The eastern extremity of the reef is marked with a single pile. Squid may be caught in this area along with pinkie snapper and other species common in Corio Bay (WGS84 ref 144 35 700 E x 38 01 850 S)

ARTHUR THE GREAT

Also within about 4.5 km of the ramp is Arthur the Great. Usually referred to as Alfred the Great by anglers of long standing; and they are probably more correct considering King Alfred was the only English Monarch to be afforded the epithet "The Great." This shallow spit and the broken ground inshore from it have long been known for good catches of whiting.

The outermost point of Arthur the Great, where it drops into deeper water, is also known for excellent catches of pinkies and good size snapper (WGS84 ref 144 33 410 E x 38 04 600 S).

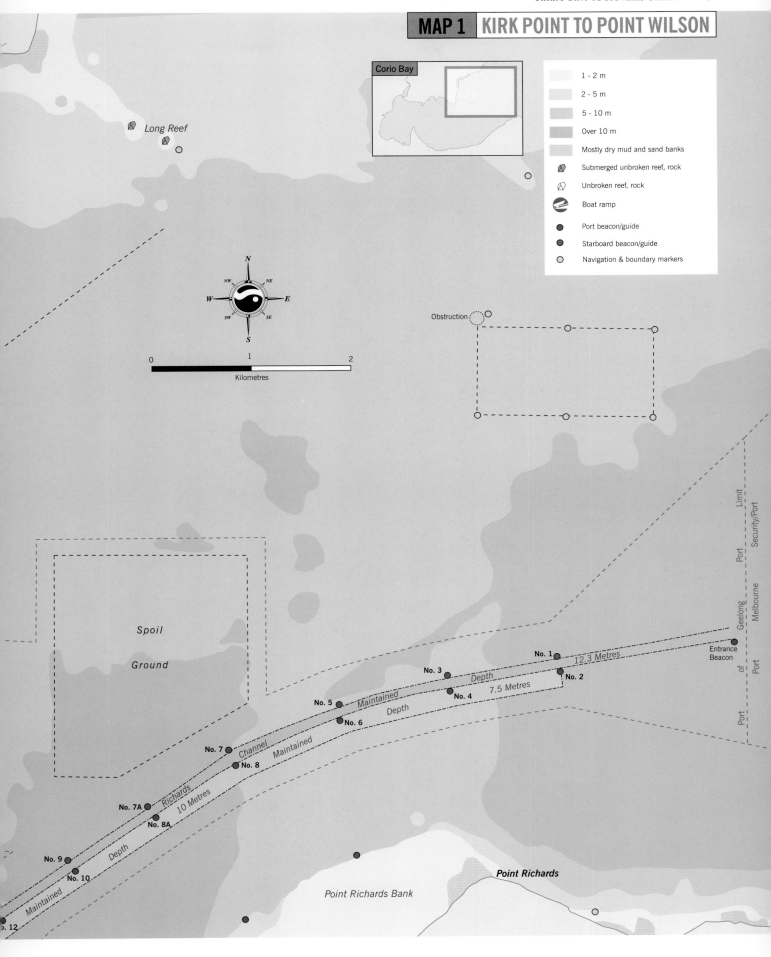

MAP 1   KIRK POINT TO POINT WILSON

Corio Bay

	1 - 2 m
	2 - 5 m
	5 - 10 m
	Over 10 m
	Mostly dry mud and sand banks

Submerged unbroken reef, rock

Unbroken reef, rock

Boat ramp

Port beacon/guide

Starboard beacon/guide

Navigation & boundary markers

Long Reef

N
NW   NE
W   E
SW   SE
S

0   1   2
Kilometres

Obstruction

Spoil

Ground

No. 1
12.3 Metres
No. 3
Depth
No. 2
7.5 Metres
No. 5
Maintained
No. 4
No. 6
Depth
No. 7
Channel
Maintained
No. 8
Richards
10 Metres
No. 7A
No. 8A
Depth
No. 9
Maintained
No. 10
No. 12

Port of Geelong   Port Security/Port Limit   Melbourne   Port of Port

Entrance
Beacon

Point Richards

Point Richards Bank

POINT LILLIAS TO AVALON

POINT LILLIAS

Taking the Avalon Beach Road exit from the Princes Highway (Melway 423 H7), after passing Dandos Road on the left and the Avalon Community on the right, turn left past the boat ramp and fishing shacks, park your car and walk in.

It takes 15 to 20 minutes from the locked gate, man-made rock barriers and deterrent signage – despite this land being permanently gazetted for public purposes – to the rocks at the water's edge from where, with a good cast, you can reach approximately four metres of water. Flathead, snapper and gummy shark have all been taken here along with several other species.

AVALON BOAT RAMP

Access to the Avalon boat ramp is from the Princes Highway and the Avalon Beach Road exit (Melway 423 H7), crossing Dandos Road then turning left toward the Avalon Shacks after passing the Avalon Community sign on the right.

The twin lane Avalon boat ramp has pontoons and mooring jetties and is near the fishermen's huts on Avalon Beach. There are toilets here but few other amenities and parking is limited. The ramp gives access to good whiting grounds in the old north channel which is marked by piles in the water more or less directly out from the ramp.

There is also access to the two embayments defined by Point Lillias and Point Wilson to the east of the ramp, but care must be taken to avoid the dangerous rocky promontory known as Bird Rock. It is clearly visible during daylight but a high tide can hide the outer fringes of this treacherous reef. Although Bird Rock appears as an island, particularly at high tide, there is no navigable passage between Bird Rock and Point Lillias.

BELOW: Corey Hargreaves with the metre long, southern blue spotted flathead he caught in Corio Bay.

The first of the embayments to the east of the Avalon ramp contains aquaculture sites which are marked with yellow buoys that flash at night. These also which define their boundaries.

These embayments are productive snapper locations (WGS84 references include 144 27 120 E x 38 05 550 S & 144 28 700 E x 38 06 020 S)

RIGHT: Avalon Boat Ramp.

FAR RIGHT: Flathead are a common catch in Corio Bay; some fish for nothing else.

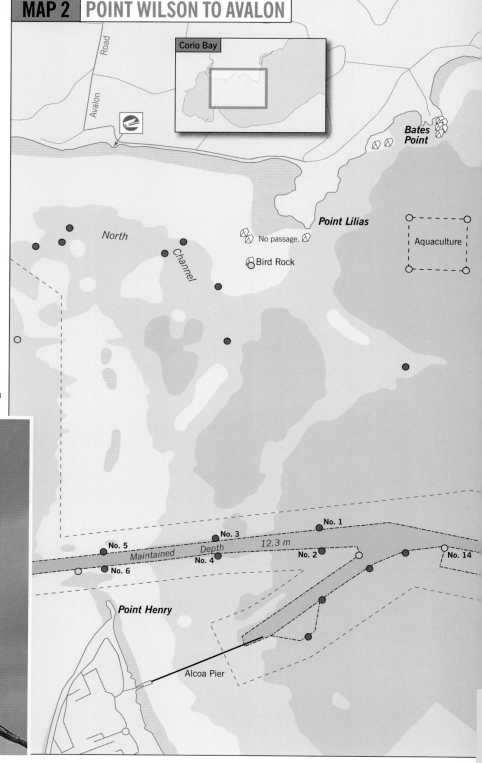

MAP 2   POINT WILSON TO AVALON

Corio Bay

Avalon Road

Bates Point

Point Lilias

North Channel

No passage.

Bird Rock

Aquaculture

No. 5

No. 6

Maintained Depth

No. 4

No. 3

12.3 m

No. 1

No. 2

No. 14

Point Henry

Alcoa Pier

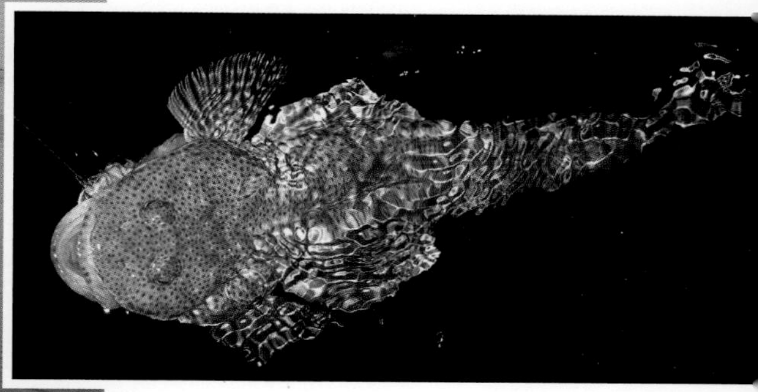

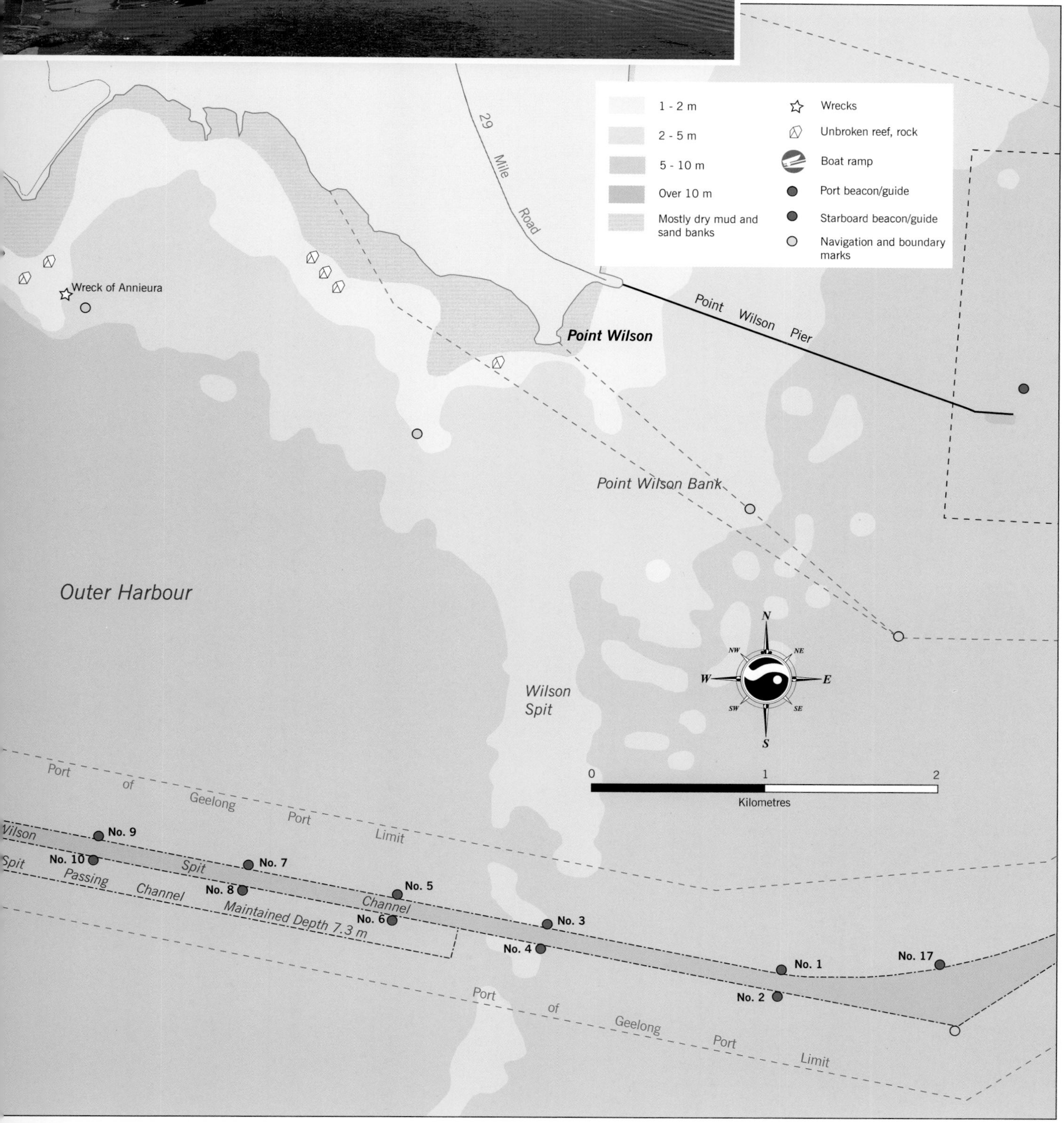

Legend

1 - 2 m	☆	Wrecks
2 - 5 m	⬡	Unbroken reef, rock
5 - 10 m		Boat ramp
Over 10 m	●	Port beacon/guide
Mostly dry mud and sand banks	●	Starboard beacon/guide
	○	Navigation and boundary marks

29 Mile Road

Wreck of Annieura

Point Wilson Pier

Point Wilson

Point Wilson Bank

Outer Harbour

Wilson Spit

N
NW NE
W E
SW SE
S

0   1   2
Kilometres

Port of Geelong Port Limit

Wilson Spit

No. 9

No. 10

Spit

No. 7

Passing Channel

No. 8

No. 5

Channel

Maintained Depth 7.3 m

No. 6

No. 3

No. 4

No. 1   No. 17

Port of Geelong Port Limit

No. 2

AVALON TO HOVELLS CREEK

LIMEBURNERS BAY

Known locally as the Grammar School Lagoon, Limeburners Bay is the estuary of Hovells Creek; a tidal lagoon which runs to sea through a narrow entrance between the Point Abeona sand spit and the beach in front of the Geelong Grammar School. Between the jetty and the bluff at the bottom of Biddlecombe Avenue the channel is up to six metres deep in places; within casting distance from the beach.

However, the lagoon itself is fairly shallow with an average depth of approximately two metres. Although this depth and sometimes greater, is maintained for some distance upstream of the many moorings, navigation should not be attempted by powered craft beyond the internal sand spit running to the north east from the site of the Lagoon Boat Club.

There is a wide variety of fish to be caught inside the lagoon including large snapper on occasions but the majority of those who fish the lagoon seek bream on light tackle. Other species to be caught within the lagoon itself include whiting, silver trevally, warehou, leatherjacket, garfish, flathead, mullet, Australian salmon and gummy shark.

BOAT LAUNCHING

You may reach Limeburners Bay by turning off the Princes Highway on School Road (Melway 432 F6), then by turning right at the roundabout, then left again once you reach Foreshore Road on which there is a modest boat ramp and car and trailer parking area just before you climb the hill to the bluff at the bottom of Biddlcombe Avenue (Melway 432 K8). The ramp gives access to productive ground between the Shell Refinery and Avalon. The shallow areas produce whiting and snapper are a good chance as well. A good spot to target them is 7 to 8 m of water out from the big Shell chimney (WGS84 ref 144 23 900 E x 38 05 550 S)

Proceeding past the beach-

ABOVE: The late Bill Sutton with a good size bream from Hovells Creek in June.

LEFT: Geoff Wilson with a good size flathead from the Point Abeona Sand Spit

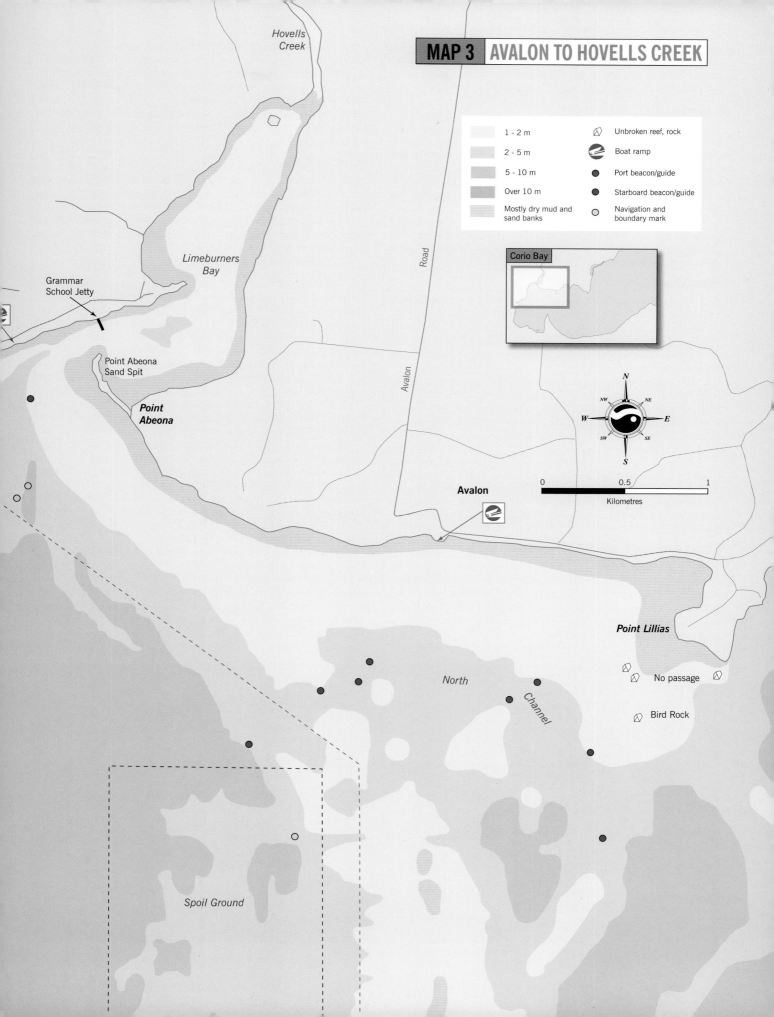

MAP 3   AVALON TO HOVELLS CREEK

Hovells
Creek

Limeburners
Bay

Grammar
School Jetty

Point Abeona
Sand Spit

**Point
Abeona**

Road

Avalon

Avalon

1 - 2 m

2 - 5 m

5 - 10 m

Over 10 m

Mostly dry mud and
sand banks

Unbroken reef, rock

Boat ramp

Port beacon/guide

Starboard beacon/guide

Navigation and
boundary mark

Corio Bay

N

NW   NE

W   E

SW   SE

S

0   0.5   1

Kilometres

Point Lillias

North

Channel

No passage

Bird Rock

Spoil Ground

facing gates of the Geelong Grammar School you will come to a short beach access track which is adjacent to the Geelong Grammar School rowing boat shed. Anglers sometimes launch small boats here, and there's a jetty to the right from which you can fish.

GRAMMAR SCHOOL JETTY

I've caught many big snapper from the jetty that this one replaced. However, the big snapper potential of this jetty has been somewhat compromised with the encroachment of completely unnecessary buoyage that is a definite hazard for anyone hooking any sort of large fish here, but the buoys don't pose a problem for those seeking whiting, Australian salmon and other more manageable species that most folk fish for here.

The biggest of many snapper I have caught from the jetty that preceded this one, and which was built in exactly the same spot, weighed 22 lb 14 oz, and was caught on May 22, 1966. Thankfully there was no buoyage around the jetty then.

GRAMMAR SCHOOL BEACH

You can no longer drive along the beach toward the bluff in front of Biddlecombe Avenue as was the case up until fairly recently. However, you can park your car, either at the jetty, or atop the rise overlooking the beach and walk to the beach. Both jetty and beach produce small Australian salmon, mullet, whiting and a variety of other species including snapper.

Most of the snapper are pinkies, but larger fish are caught here from time to time, particularly from the end of March until the end of September. Keep in mind; you do need to be prepared to spend a good deal of time to have a realistic chance of catching a big one. An incoming tide between midnight and dawn has produced many for me over the years.

For the majority of species, including snapper, the most productive time to fish both the jetty and the beach is during the first couple of hours of the rising tide. This enhanced period of good fishing begins between four and five hours after the advertised time of low water at Port Phillip Heads, so do the calculations to get the best results.

POINT ABEONA SAND SPIT

There was a time when you could walk the entire length of the Point Abeona Sand Spit after parking at the bottom of Avalon Beach Road. Alas that is no longer an option because the sand spit has been badly eroded in the past two and a half decades and the only access is by boat. Even then you can only fish the tip of the spit from approximately half ebb to half flood.

Species to be caught here are the same as the beach and jetty in

front of the Grammar School, but good size bream may be caught here more readily than at the former locations. Casting distance is shorter and there are fewer problems with strong tides and drifting weed. My biggest bream from here weighed 1.65 kg in September 1998. I also caught my largest snapper from Corio Bay here, officially weighed in at 23 lb 13 oz on September 6, 1962 and was a record at the Geelong and District Angling Club of which I was a member at the time.

HOVELLS CREEK

Hovells Creek is rarely fished these days but it contains good size bream and has done so for as long as I can remember. My late friend Bill Sutton caught some beauties there but access is limited.

Hovells Creek may be accessed by small rowing boat or canoe from Limeburners Bay. However, the entrance is shallow and at low tide may not be accessible.

The following are the current options:

FISHING PLATFORM

There is a wooden platform that offers angler's access from the shared walking/cycling track that runs from the end of Foreshore Road just past the Lagoon Boat Club (Melway Page 11 C14). This track continues several kilometres right up to the Princes Highway (Melway 423 D10) but the platform is situated a short distance above the entrance to Limeburners Bay, a distance of 1.4 km, and for me, a 25 minute walk from where you can park your car just past the Lagoon Boat Club.

The channel in the creek is on the opposite side to the platform and a fair cast is required to reach productive water. However, there are some good size bream to be caught here by competent anglers.

In my youth, the Hovells Creek estuary extended for quite some distance above the Princes Highway and it was this upper section known as the Duck Ponds that produced trophy size bream. Unfortunately, the powers that be had the creek dammed just above the highway so that fishery was lost. However, bream may still be caught as far upstream as the pool just downstream from the Bridge over the Princes Highway (Melway 423 D10) despite the usually unattractive appearance of the water here.

The shared track may also be accessed above the halfway mark from Cummins Road (Melway 432 K2) .

Hovells Creek may be accessed from the Princes Highway, Corio. Take the North Shore exit (Melway 432 K1), into Shell Parade then Cummins Road to the high ground overlooking the creek. The escarpment above the creek is fenced off from the shared access track and bank access is minimal between the highway and Limeburners Bay.

ABOVE: Travis Bauer and Arie De Wit with a mixed bag of garfish and pinkies from the Grammar School Lagoon.

ABOVE: Ivan Bereza with a snapper of 8.5 kg from Corio Bay's inner harbour.

CHAPTER 2
NORTH SHORE ROCKS TO POINT HENRY

ABOVE: Paul Mayer with a nice snapper taken from the rocks at St Helens.

NORTH SHORE ROCKS TO POINT HENRY

NORTH SHORE ROCKS

The North Shore Rocks are in the Geelong suburb of North Shore and extend from the Phosphate Company weighbridge (Melway 442 F2) to Moorpanyal Park (Melway 442 E3)

The platforms below the weighbridge are fishable on all tides, but you can only fish from the other rocks, those around to the right hand side toward Corio Quay, when the tide is out.

Grass whiting, may be caught here using sandworms for bait while large King George whiting often give the angler a pleasant surprise. Casting out with large baits like pilchards will occasionally tempt a snapper, but small flathead and undersize pinkie snapper can be a nuisance here.

The North Shore Rocks are also a noted location for lure-casting enthusiasts seeking large snook. In my experience October is the most productive month but they may be present here any time from the end of August until mid November.

The rocks below the escarpment between Moorpanyal Park and Corio Quay North extension (once the site of Fletchers Jetty) can produce large snapper for the dedicated angler.

WINTER SNAPPER

Anglers fishing from boats in front of the North Shore Rocks and Corio Quay during winter pick up some large snapper with most captures being taken after dark. However, they are present in good numbers some years, and other years they are few and far between.

The Queens Birthday Weekend in June is a noted time for big snapper here but they may be caught from April to September when rising water temperatures usually mobilize them for parts unknown. There is generally a fresh run of fish in October that are far easier to catch than the fish that have wintered in the bay.

The most productive technique for locating snapper during winter is to simply drive around slowly whilst looking at the sounder because they tend to group in tight pods and not move around much because the cold water temperatures, down to 9 degrees, do not fully support their metabolism. Having located a pod of fish, the angler has to persuade them to take a bait; not always an easy task because they do not feed as actively with water temperatures low and falling.

MACKEY STREET ROCKS

The Mackey Street Rocks may be accessed via road by either turning off the Princes Highway, North Geelong at Mackey Street (Melway 442 A7), or from Corio Quay Road via McLeod Street (Melway 442 A6).

You may drive out onto the reclaimed land and fish from either the rock groyne or from the small timber platforms there. From the rock groyne, snapper are the main species sought but flathead and small pinkie snapper are the main catch from here. Garfish are sometimes taken from the adjacent wooden platforms.

ABOVE: Anglers fishing from one of the new platforms below the old weighbridge in front of Incitec Pivot.

St Helens boat ramp

The twin lane boat launching facility at the bottom of Swinburne Street in North Geelong (Melway 442 B8) has adequate parking, boat washing facilities, a fish cleaning table and toilets. A launching fee is payable and collected by the Geelong branch of the Australian Volunteer Coastguard which is based here.

St Helens ramp provides access to the whole of Corio Bay but experience has shown that you don't need to go far to catch a snapper. The ground in front of the old Wheat Pier and on the east side of the Corio Channel is well worth persisting with late into the night (WGS84 ref 144 22 400 E x 38 07 000 S).

There are good whiting grounds to the south, extending past the site of the old Tug Pier (which replaced Huttons Jetty back in the 50's) to Western Beach, to the Western Beach mornings and to the north in front of Moorpanyal Park North Shore.

Land based Access

St Helens is also a popular spot for land based anglers. Here, anglers may fish from the reclaimed land with the benefit of being able to watch there rods from their cars. A variety of fish are caught here including flathead and the occasional snapper. Sandworms fished in close will sometimes produce a good size bream or two but leatherjackets, small pinkie snapper and small whiting are more common.

St Helens Jetty

This jetty replaced the old swimming enclosure at St Helens and is located at the southern end of the reclaimed land, just past the children's playground. It was intended as a swimmers jetty and has a sign on it banning fishing. However, unlike the old swimming baths it replaced, it is a very rare sight to see anybody swimming there because it is not an enclosed area and people fish there.

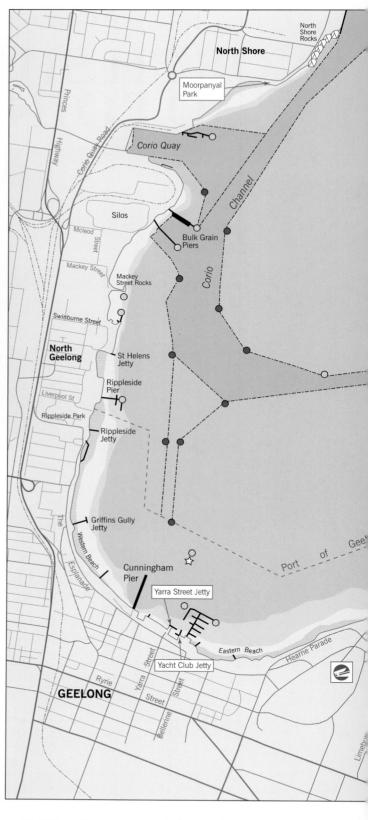

St Helens Jetty produces flathead, silver trevally, whiting, garfish, and the occasional snapper amongst the usual undersize pinkies and small flathead.

The Tug Pier

There is no public access to the old tug pier at the bottom of Liverpool Street in North Geelong. This area has been earmarked for residential development despite limited road access.

MAP 4 | NORTH SHORE ROCKS TO POINT HENRY

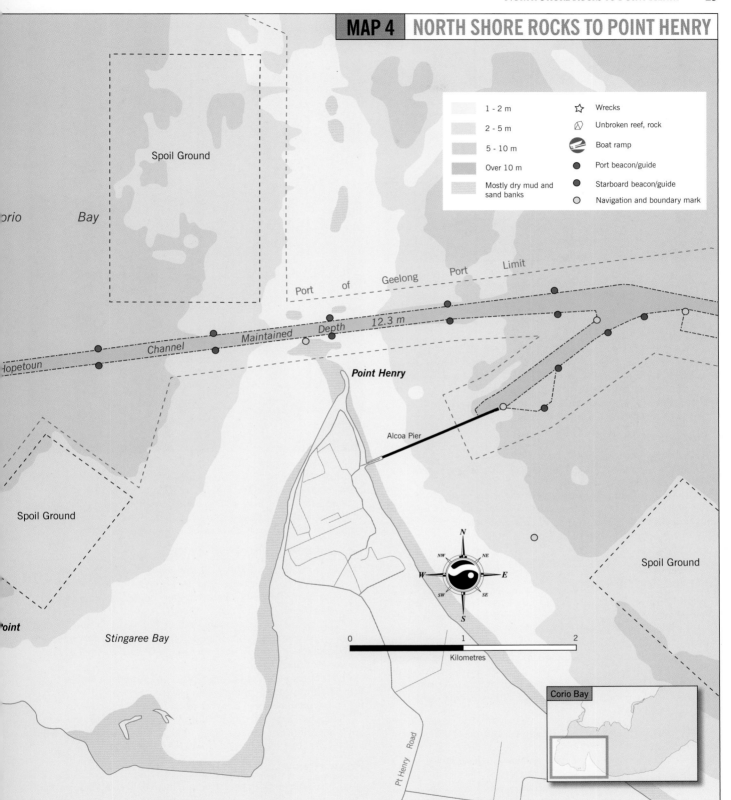

1 - 2 m	☆	Wrecks
2 - 5 m	⬡	Unbroken reef, rock
5 - 10 m		Boat ramp
Over 10 m	●	Port beacon/guide
Mostly dry mud and sand banks	●	Starboard beacon/guide
	○	Navigation and boundary mark

Spoil Ground

orio   Bay

Port   of   Geelong   Port   Limit

Hopetoun   Channel   Maintained   Depth   12.3 m

Point Henry

Alcoa Pier

Spoil Ground

Spoil Ground

Point

Stingaree Bay

N
NW   NE
W   E
SW   SE
S

0   1   2
Kilometres

Pt Henry Road

Corio Bay

RIPPLESIDE JETTY

Rippleside Jetty is reached by turning off the Princes Highway at Bell Parade, Drumcondra (Melway 441 K10), then into Rippleside Park to the left from where it is a short walk to the jetty.

Good catches of King George whiting and garfish are taken here on light tackle at times, while a large bait cast right out will occasionally tempt a nice flathead or snapper.

GRIFFINS GULLY JETTY

This popular jetty (Melway 442 A12) is accessible from The Esplanade at the beginning of Western Beach. Travelling south, the turn-off is on the left, having passed Toorak Pde and the Chifley motel on the right.

Fish caught from here include whiting and flathead. As is the case with Rippleside jetty, a long cast can sometimes produce a

Steve Rayson and Alec Phipps with their snapper catch from Corio Bay.

Rod Butcher with a spotted ling from the Geelong Waterfront.

decent snapper, particularly during the early hours of the morning, but due to the overly close encroachment of moorings in front of the jetty this option has become increasingly problematic.

WESTERN BEACH WALL

Extending from the boat building sheds at Western Beach to Cunningham Pier; the Western Beach retaining wall is accessible from the Foreshore Reserve at the base of Cunningham Pier (Melway 401 H2). It provides good fishing for legal size pinkie snapper and the occasional bigger fish to those able to cast a reasonable distance. Other species taken here include whiting, bream and silver trevally.

CUNNINGHAM PIER

Located at the junction of Western and Eastern Beach Roads (Melway 452 B3), Cunningham Pier is a mecca, both for young anglers and those of more senior years.

Mullet and flathead are the main fish caught from the pier, however leatherjacket, silver trevally, warehou (or snotty trevalla), slimy mackerel and barracouta are all taken here at times; some right down beside the piles of the pier.

Cunningham Pier is now privately owned and access is restricted to mainly daylight hours and evening.

GEELONG WATERFRONT

Extending from Cunningham Pier to the Geelong Yacht Club, the Geelong Waterfront is a favourite haunt for lure fishermen – most of them soft plastics exponents – seeking mainly pinkie snapper and occasionally picking up a larger specimen. Other species caught here include bream, warehou and flathead. Among the most popular places to fish here are the platform in front of the Carousel, the Alexander Thompson Jetty nearby and the mooring enclosure between the Fishermen's Pier restaurant and the Geelong Yacht Club.

BOAT HIRE

Fishing boats are for hire at the Geelong Waterfront.
Phone 5222 3222 or 0414 599 363.
Email *rentatinny@bigpond.com.au* or visit *www.rentatinny.com.au*

YARRA STREET

The jetty and rock groyne complex at the bottom of Yarra Street (Melway 228 D1) is not fished heavily but leatherjacket, mullet, silver trevally, mackerel and salmon have all been taken in good numbers, along with the occasional snapper and various other species.

Access to rocks at the bottom of Yarra Street is restricted when the helipad is in use but there are places to fish in close proximity.

YACHT CLUB JETTY

Located between the bottom of Bellerine and Yarra Streets, and adjacent to the Geelong Yacht Club, this jetty, adjacent moorings, and the rock groyne protruding from the left hand side are favoured areas for soft plastic enthusiasts; the rock groyne in particular.

Species caught here include silver trevally, warehou, pinkie snapper and flathead, but as is the case with other inshore locations; larger fish, including snapper, are sometimes taken from here.

LIMEBURNERS POINT BOAT RAMP

The boat launching facility at the end of Hearne Parade at Limeburners Point (Melway 452 H2), gives boats to six metres access to Corio Bay. Land based anglers sometimes fish from the sheltering breakwaters.

Whiting are sometimes caught here, but small flathead would be the most common catch. Snapper are occasionally taken here at dawn or dusk, and following very rough weather, particularly from the north or north east.

Limeburners Point boat ramp gives access to the whole of Corio Bay. There are good whiting grounds within Stingaree Bay which is the embayment between Limeburners Point and Point Henry.

Snapper may be caught within a kilometre of the ramp anywhere north of an imaginary line joining Limeburners Point and Point Henry (WGS84 ref 144 23 400 E x 38 08 000 S).

POINT HENRY

Small boats may be launched from the sand on the east side of Point Henry, just north of the Alcoa Pier giving access to productive whiting grounds either side of the Alcoa Pier (Melway 454 F2).

Garfish are also a good proposition here along with yellowtail kingfish which may be caught in the vicinity of the Alcoa pier from late summer to early autumn. Live garfish are the most effective baits here and early morning is the best time for the exercise.

Serious contenders for this exercise may launch from Limeburners Point prior to dawn. With a spotlight and dip-net you can catch garfish that can be kept alive for the operation which involves trolling them slowly along the conveyor side of the pier.

CHAPTER 3
CLIFTON SPRINGS TO STEELES ROCKS

BELLARINE PENINSULA

Geelong is the Gateway to the Bellarine Peninsula and Port Phillip Heads. However most of the fishing is done from boats; there are few spots from which you can fish Corio Bay land based along that section of the peninsula which skirts the outer harbour.

CURLEWIS BANK TO POINT RICHARDS

CLIFTON SPRINGS BOAT RAMP

The Clifton Springs boat launching facility at the end of Jetty Road (Melway ref 456 E5) is adequate for boats to six metres, although some difficulties have been experienced at low tide. Facilities include a fish cleaning table and toilet block

The ramp is protected by a seawall from which anglers sometimes fish, both on the outside, and within the harbour itself. The water is fairly shallow but some good size flathead have been caught here by lure fishing enthusiasts, mainly with the soft plastics. High tide seems to be the best time for this exercise; particularly should you be fishing the outside of the wall.

The Clifton Springs boat ramp provides access to both the Point Richards and Wilson Spit Channels, along the edges of which good size snapper may be taken, particularly from October through until at least the end of March.

Whiting and squid are abundant here at times as well, with good catches of both being taken more or less straight out from the ramp in two to five metres of water.

THE TURN

The junction of the Point Richards and Wilson Spit Channels is known by most who fish from boat, as "The Turn". Located about 3.5 km NW of the ramp; it's a favourite snapper fishing location and it's rare not to see a few boats anchored there (WGS84 ref 144 32 150 E x 38 07 900 S).

THE SPOIL GROUND

The edge of the spoil ground off Curlewis is a productive spot for snapper with the best chance of success at dawn or dusk and following either tide change (WGS84 ref 144 27 900 E x 38 08 200 S).

WILSON SPIT

Along the edges of the shipping channels are good places to fish for snapper. Where the Wilson Spit Channel cuts through the spit itself at markers three and four is a particularly good place to fish the side of the channel fished being dependant on wind direction.

Additional marks to fish along the edge of the Wilson Spit include Wilson Spit North (WGS84 ref 144 30 120 E x 38 07 200 S) and Wilson Spit South (WGS84 REF 144 30 000 E x 38 07 950 S).

BEACON POINT

Beacon Point (Melway 457 A2) is located at the bottom of Beacon Point Road Clifton Springs. The beach is accessible by a flight of stairs from where you can park your car on the grassy verge above.

Anglers that wade the shallows catch flathead here on lures during the warmer weather, and while it's rare to get a really big

one, fish of a kilogram or so are a fairly common catch.

Fishing boats are available for hire at Clifton Springs. For more information phone Mike on 0409 028 454.

FRESHWATER OPTIONS

McLeods Waterholes on Wyndham Street running off the east side of Jetty Road (Melway 456 G10) and Lake Lorne near the old Drysdale railway station (Melway 456 F12) contain a variety of fish including golden perch and roach. Shrimp and small fish may be dip netted for bait down beside bank side foliage. However, European carp dominate angler's catches from these waters during the day, and eels come on the bite after dark.

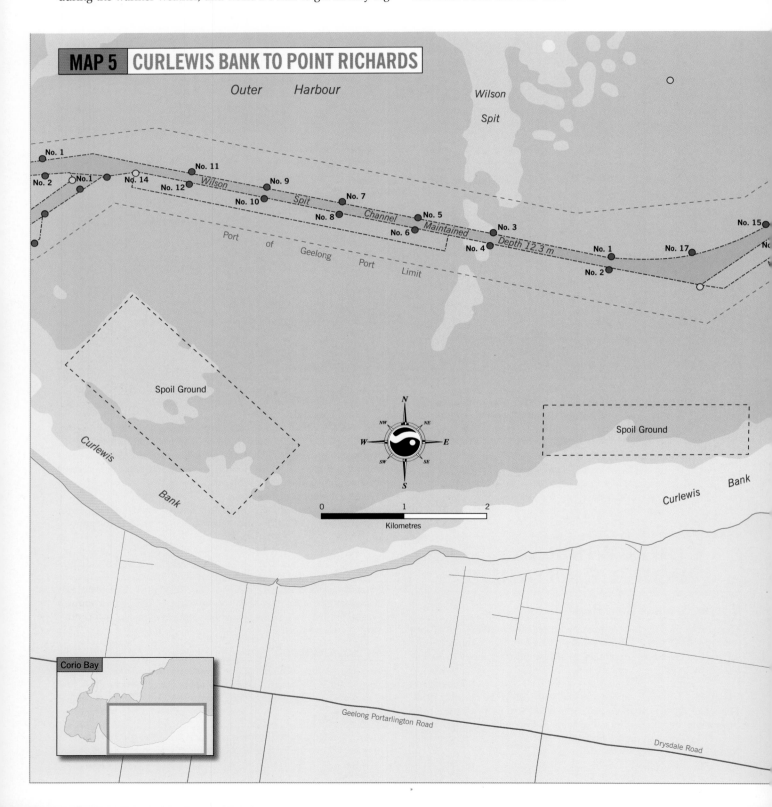

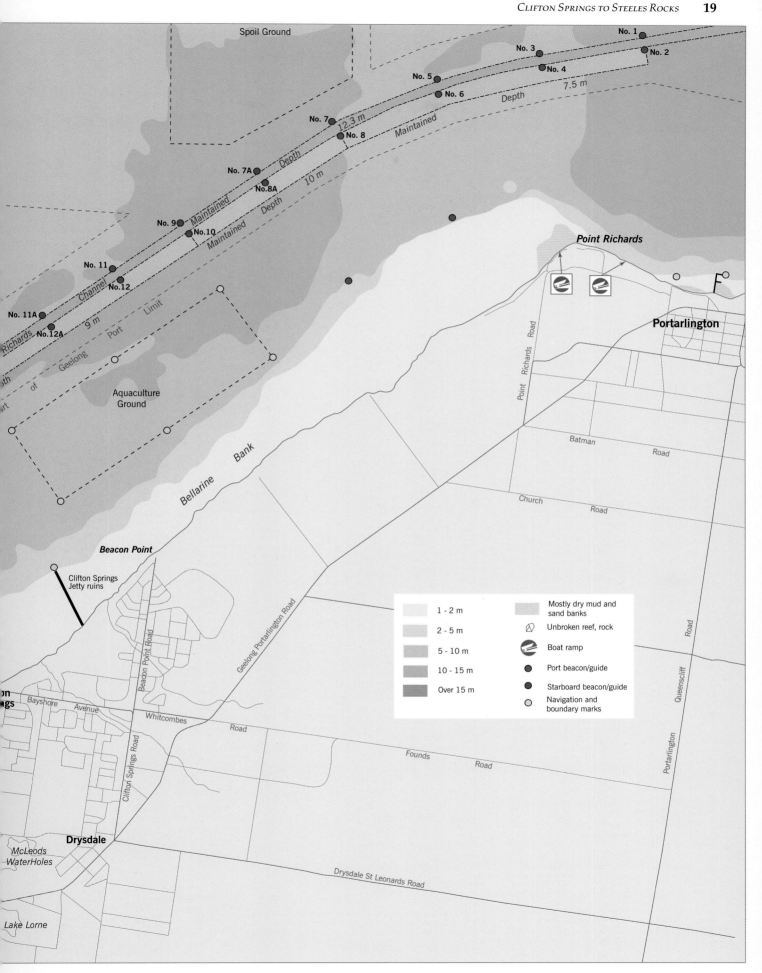

Spoil Ground

No. 1
No. 3
No. 2
No. 4
No. 5
No. 6
7.5 m
Depth
Maintained
No. 7
12.3 m
No. 8
Maintained Depth
No. 7A
No.8A
10 m
Maintained Depth
No. 9
No.10
Maintained
No. 11
Channel
No.12
No. 11A
Richards
9 m
Port
No.12A
Geelong
Limit
of
Aquaculture
Ground

Bellarine
Bank

Point Richards

Portarlington

Point Richards Road

Batman
Road

Church
Road

Beacon Point

Clifton Springs
Jetty ruins

Beacon Point Road

Geelong Portarlington Road

Queenscliff Road

Portarlington

on
gs

Bayshore
Avenue

Whitcombes
Road

	1 - 2 m		Mostly dry mud and sand banks
	2 - 5 m	⬡	Unbroken reef, rock
	5 - 10 m		Boat ramp
	10 - 15 m	●	Port beacon/guide
	Over 15 m	●	Starboard beacon/guide
		○	Navigation and boundary marks

Founds
Road

Drysdale

McLeods
WaterHoles

Drysdale St Leonards Road

Lake Lorne

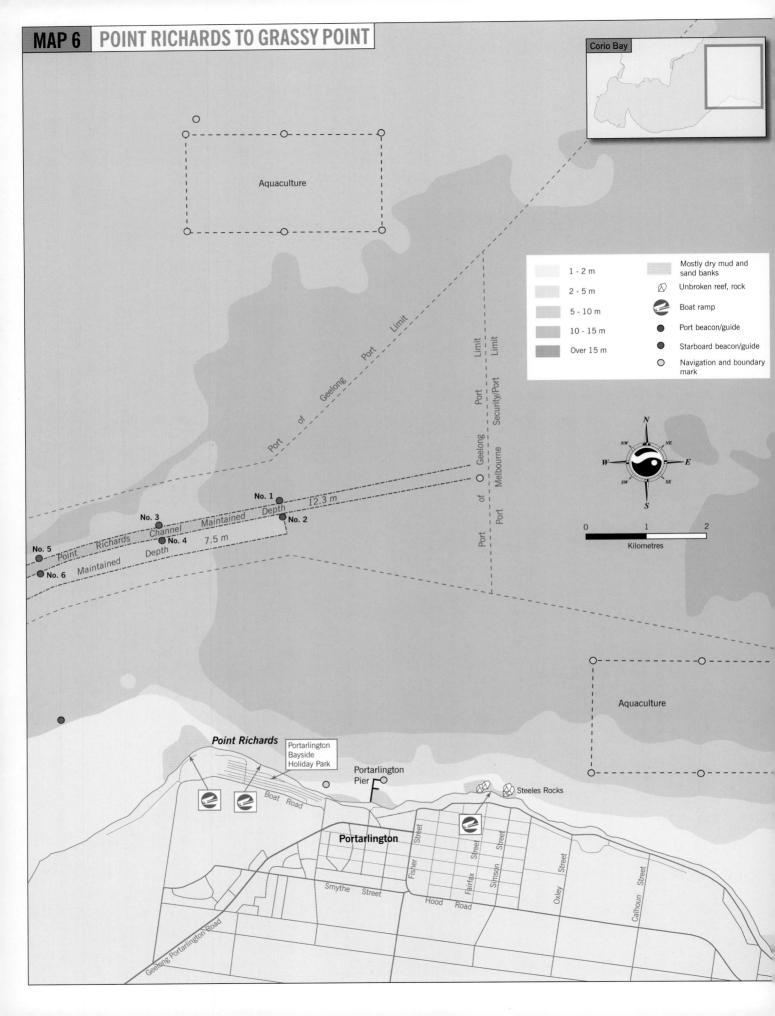

MAP 6 — POINT RICHARDS TO GRASSY POINT

Corio Bay

Aquaculture

Legend:
- 1 - 2 m
- 2 - 5 m
- 5 - 10 m
- 10 - 15 m
- Over 15 m
- Mostly dry mud and sand banks
- Unbroken reef, rock
- Boat ramp
- Port beacon/guide
- Starboard beacon/guide
- Navigation and boundary mark

Port of Geelong Port Limit

Port of Geelong Port Limit

Port of Melbourne Port Security/Port Limit

No. 1
No. 2
No. 3
No. 4
No. 5
No. 6

12.3 m

Point Richards Channel Maintained Depth

7.5 m

Maintained Depth

N
NW NE
W E
SW SE
S

0 1 2
Kilometres

Aquaculture

Point Richards

Portarlington Bayside Holiday Park

Portarlington Pier

Steeles Rocks

Boat Road

Portarlington

Fisher Street
Fairfax Street
Simson Street
Oxley Street
Calhoun Street

Smythe Street

Hood Road

Geelong Portarlington Road

POINT RICHARDS TO GRASSY POINT

POINT RICHARDS BOAT RAMP

There is an excellent four lane boat launching facility at Point Richards with adequate parking on all but public holidays during good weather. (Melway 444 C4). There is a sheltering breakwater and mooring jetties catering for boats to six metres or so with a clearly marked passage to the sea. However, difficulties may be experienced on the very lowest of tides.

CARAVAN PARK BOAT RAMP

There is another excellent four lane boat ramp within the Portarlington Bayside Holiday Park at the bottom of Boat Avenue (Melway 444 D5), which may be used by both park residents and the public. However, members of the public are required to purchase a yearly permit.

Further information is available on line at *info@bellarinebayside. com.au* and *www.bellarinebayside.com.au* on 03 5259 2764, or Free Call: 1800 222 778.

THE OLD CHANNEL

The north side of the shipping channel, between beacons three and five and almost due north from the Point Richards boat ramp, is a well-known snapper mark and boats congregate here from September onwards with the realistic expectation of catching a snapper or two.

After crossing the shipping channel, the ground rises to eight metres or so and when it drops into 10 or 11 m you have reached the old shipping channel. (WGS84 ref 144 37 200 E x 38 05 200 S)

Whiting are also present in good numbers within a kilometre or so of the Point Richards ramp, the imperative being the presence of weed patches and visibly broken ground.

PORTARLINGTON PIER

Portarlington pier (Melway ref 444 H6) is now a secure boat harbour with a protecting stone breakwater extending to the east from the original structure. Whiting are sometimes caught from the pier, along with Australian salmon, flathead and squid. Local mussel farmers also sell their produce from boats moored alongside the pier.

The breakwater itself does not receive a lot of attention from anglers but it has produced pinkies and good size snapper at dawn and dusk, as well as during, and immediately after, a blow from the north or north east strong enough to heavily discolour the water.

Access is provided by a footpath along its length and anglers can fish from the sloping stone wall where a fairly comfortable position is not hard to find.

STEELES ROCKS

There is a modest boat ramp suitable for trailer boats to 4.5 m at Steeles Rocks just below the reserve at the bottom of Fairfax Street, but difficulties may be experienced at low tide (Melway ref 445 A5).

Submerged rocks, particularly on the right hand side of the boat ramp and extending further out than those visible above the surface, can prove a navigation hazard so take care.

Squid and whiting are the main species sought by anglers launching boats here, but from around the first week in November, good size pinkie snapper move onto the heavy ground from about 350 m offshore between Oxley and Calhoun Streets and just inshore the aquaculture zone around to the right. The most productive times to fish for them here is from very first light until an hour after sunrise, and again from an hour before sunset until just after dark.

Partially exposed at low tide, Steeles Rocks provide a marginal platform for land based anglers seeking squid and garfish, and in spring time snook on lures at dawn and dusk. You have to traverse submerged ground to reach the end of the promontory here which

ABOVE: The breakwater section of the Portarlington Pier is a good spot to try for snapper at dawn or dusk.

drops away into about three metres of water. The ground is too foul for bottom fishing though.

I noticed at the time of writing, the usual access point at the bottom of Simson Street, along with a good portion of the adjoining shoreline, was in the process of being fenced off, for what one can only assume are safety concerns over the crumbling escarpment so you may need to find access along the beach to fish here.

Bass yabbies may be pumped from the mud and sand between the Portarlington Pier and Steeles Rocks provided the tide has fallen far enough to expose their holes.

RIGHT: Simon Werner with a 9.5 kg snapper from the deep mud off Portarlington.

BELOW: Steeles Rocks Boat Ramp at Portarlington.

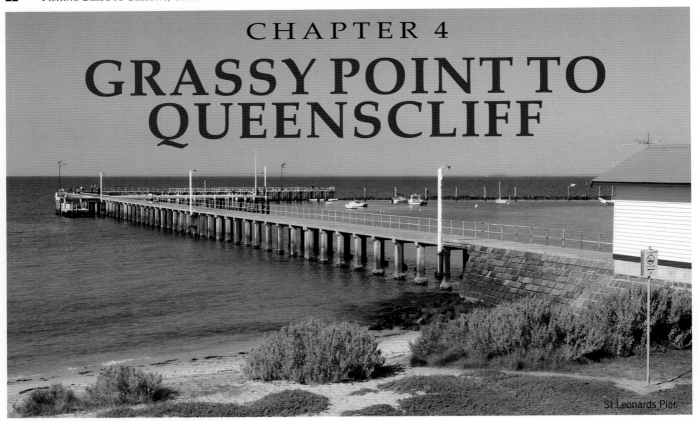

St Leonards Pier.

CHAPTER 4
GRASSY POINT TO QUEENSCLIFF

GRASSY POINT TO ST LEONARDS

GRASSY POINT

Grassy Point is one of the best known whiting and squid producing areas on the Bellarine Peninsula. The modest boat ramp at the bottom of Grassy Point Road (Melway 445 G8) allows small boats to be launched and retrieved in respect to the tide cycle.

Whiting are usually plentiful at the edge of the mussel leases just offshore, and squid are usually plentiful over the inshore reef patches and visible grass beds.

INDENTED HEAD

There is an adequate, twin-lane, boat ramp at Indented Head (Melway 460 C3) with adequate parking on all but public holidays in good weather. There is a jetty suitable for short term mooring but not much apart from that.

There is a good deal of shallow reef near the ramp including the inner and outer Governor reefs which are close to the ramp on the right hand side, all of which are appropriately marked.

Squid and whiting are the main species caught off Indented Head but in spring, large snook may be taken trolling lures or drifting with bait over the seagrass areas out on the Prince George Bank. Good size flathead may be taken as well, both in the shallows and out deep. Best advice is to fish the very edge of the Prince George Bank on the drift during the rising tide.

Boats may be hired at Beachlea Boat Hire at Shed 8 on the Indented Head Foreshore. For booking, phone Rod on 0403 890 565.

THE DEEP MUD

Heading due east from the Indented Head Ramp for six kilometres or so you will reach the deep mud in about 22 m of water. This is an excellent area to sit out in the daytime for big snapper, particularly over the high tide change. They seem to be present out here during the December/January period when they have gone quiet just about everywhere else (WGS84 ref 144 47 500 E x 38 08 700 S).

ST LEONARDS BOAT RAMP

The four lane St Leonards boat ramp at the bottom of Leviens Road (Melway ref 460 B12) is suitable for all trailer boats with due regard for the tide cycle but is exposed to easterly and north easterly winds and swell. The twin ramps are separated by a well-appointed mooring jetty.

There is usually adequate parking except during good weather, particularly on public holidays, when the car park fills quickly. At present, cars and trailers can park on the vacant land on the opposite side of The Esplanade, but that situation may not be permanent.

ST LEONARDS PIER

The pier at St Leonards (Melway ref 460 C9), has gained a deserved reputation for producing both snapper (to those prepared to put in the time) and squid.

Sadly, the breakwater section of the pier has fallen into a state of disrepair and is no longer safe to fish from. In the most productive location, anglers have to climb down from the pier onto the remainder of the breakwater to secure any large snapper they might have hooked because the wooden structure of the pier no longer extends to the edge of the breakwater.

The squid are caught at night as a rule, so too are the snapper, but a strong northerly or north easterly will sometimes bring snapper on the bite here during the day.

WHITING

Like Indented Head, most who launch from St Leonards are seeking whiting and squid which are available within a short distance of the ramp. Whiting marks aren't set in stone, so prospecting for visibly clear patches among the darker patches of weed is an important skill for those seeking whiting, both here and elsewhere.

You will very likely see clusters of boats on the better known whiting marks including one known as Bourke Street a few hundred metres out from the ramp and further south.

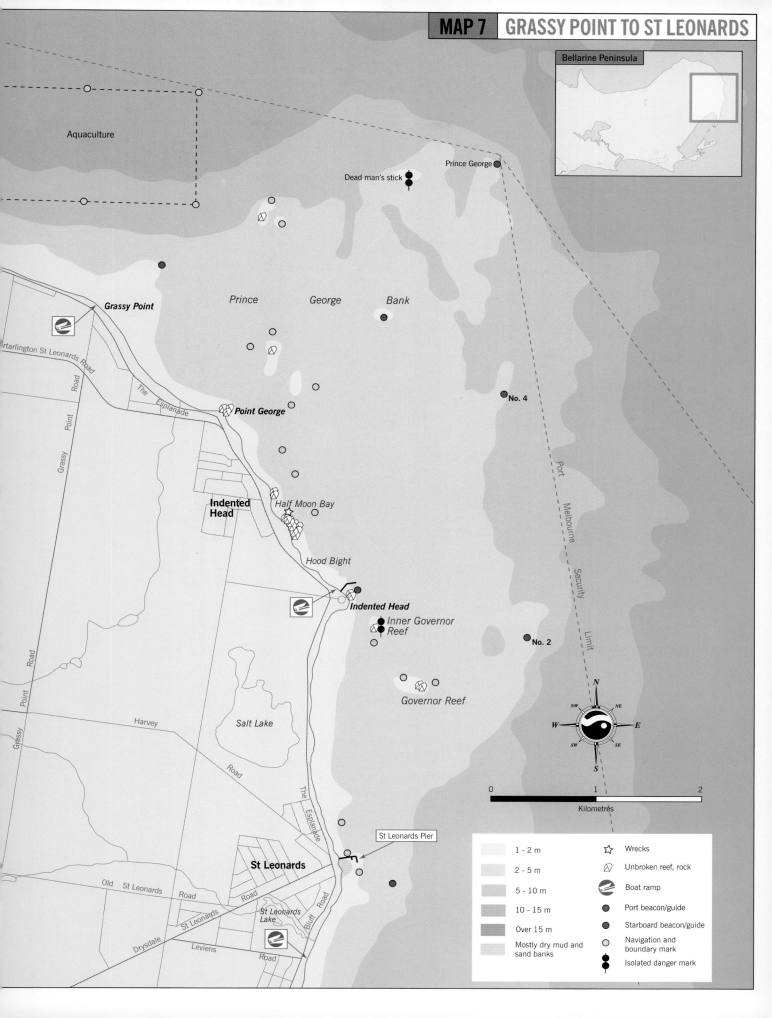

MAP 7 GRASSY POINT TO ST LEONARDS

Bellarine Peninsula

Aquaculture

Dead man's stick

Prince George

Grassy Point

Prince   George   Bank

artarlington St Leonards Road

Grassy Point Road

The Esplanade

Point George

No. 4

Indented Head

Half Moon Bay

Hood Bight

Indented Head

Inner Governor Reef

No. 2

Governor Reef

Grassy Point Road

Harvey

Salt Lake

Road

The Esplanade

Port Melbourne Security Limit

N
NW   NE
W   E
SW   SE
S

St Leonards Pier

St Leonards

Old   St Leonards   Road

Road

St Leonards Lake

Bluff Road

Drysdale   Leviens   Road

0	1	2

Kilometres

1 - 2 m	☆ Wrecks
2 - 5 m	⬡ Unbroken reef, rock
5 - 10 m	🛥 Boat ramp
10 - 15 m	● Port beacon/guide
Over 15 m	● Starboard beacon/guide
Mostly dry mud and sand banks	○ Navigation and boundary mark
	● Isolated danger mark

ST LEONARDS TO QUEENSCLIFF

COLES CHANNEL

Coles Channel, which is the closest channel to shore off St Leonards, is well regarded whiting ground, particularly the area offshore from The Bluff at the bottom of Gilbert Street and further south off the St Leonards Yacht Club.

After dark, the Coles Channel is well known for producing good size gummy shark and the occasional snapper.

WEST CHANNEL

Clearly marked by the West Channel Pile visible from the shore, and to the SSE by red and green buoys, the West Channel is the next channel encountered when travelling to the south east from St Leonards. It is a prohibited anchorage under Port Rule 62A. However, the edges of the West Channel produce good catches of whiting under suitable conditions.

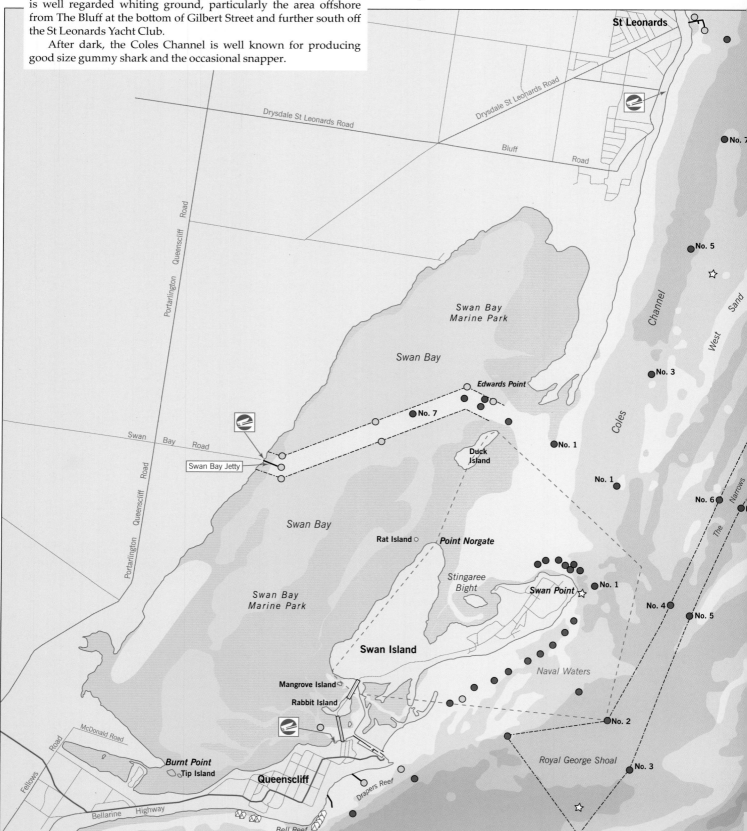

THE DEEP MUD

Heading due east from the St Leonards Ramp for eight kilometres or so you will reach the deep mud in 23 m of water (WGS84 ref 144 48 500 E x 38 10 800 S). This is an excellent area to sit out in the daytime for a big snapper, particularly over the high tide change, and during the December/January period when they seem to have gone quiet just about everywhere else.

WRECK OF THE CLARENCE

South of St Leonards in approximately 4.5 m of water, lies the Wreck of the Clarence which is off limits to both divers and fishermen because of its fragile state, however from the Clarence wreck, south to the entrance of Swan Bay is some of the best whiting and squid ground to be found on the Bellarine Peninsula (WGS84 ref 144 43 160 E x 38 12 140 S).

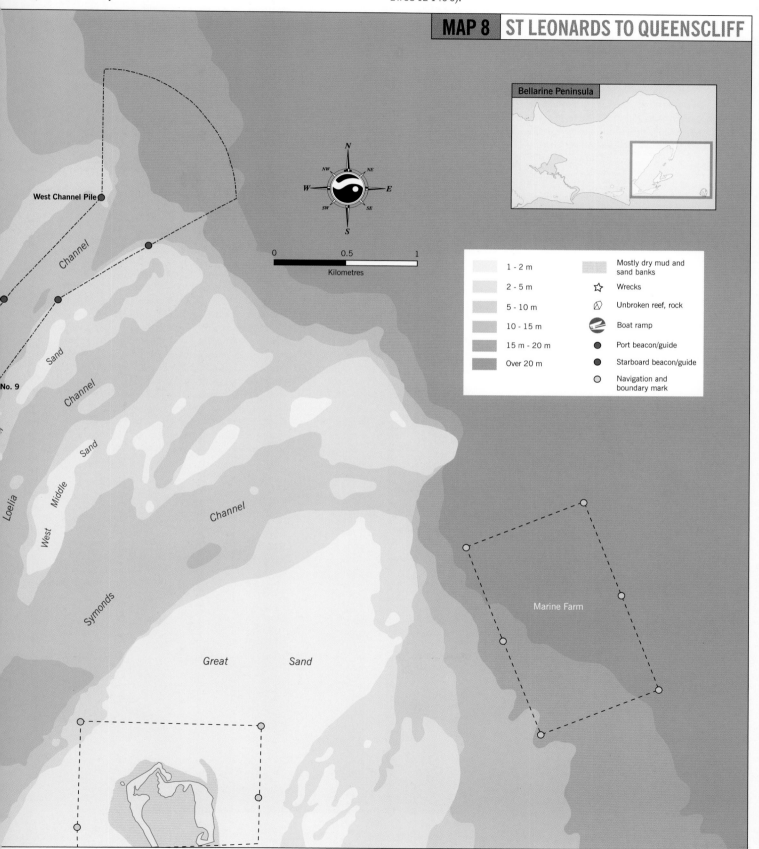

MAP 8 **ST LEONARDS TO QUEENSCLIFF**

Bellarine Peninsula

West Channel Pile

Channel

Sand

Channel

No. 9

Loelia

West

Middle

Sand

Symonds

Channel

Great   Sand

Marine Farm

N
NW   NE
W   E
SW   SE
S

0   0.5   1
Kilometres

	1 - 2 m	
	2 - 5 m	
	5 - 10 m	
	10 - 15 m	
	15 m - 20 m	
	Over 20 m	

Mostly dry mud and sand banks

☆ Wrecks

Unbroken reef, rock

Boat ramp

Port beacon/guide

Starboard beacon/guide

Navigation and boundary mark

SWAN BAY

The entrance of Swan Bay is well regarded ground for producing whiting, garfish and squid along with the occasional good size gummy shark. However, most of Swan Bay itself has been declared a marine park where you are not allowed to fish. You can fish from the jetty and along the marked channel and in other areas that are outside the boundaries.

There are big flathead to be caught in Swan Bay over the warmer months of the year, along with gummy shark, bream and several other species. Gummy shark may be caught in the deep channel that runs in close beside Duck Island but large rays are attracted to fleshy baits that anglers use to attract gummies.

Swan Bay boat ramp.

JETTY

There is a modest boat ramp and a jetty at the end of Swan Bay Road (Melway ref 486 H1). Although the water around the jetty is shallow, it may produce the occasional flathead during the day and gummy shark at night, but the main species to be caught from here are small whiting and garfish.

In the past, tailor has been known to herd baitfish under the jetty on evening, but this is something we have not witnessed for some years now. Never the less, tailor are sometimes encountered at the mouth of Swan Bay so that fishery may remain a possibility for the future.

SWAN BAY BOAT RAMP

There is a boat ramp at the base of the Swan Bay Jetty that accommodates small craft with respect to the tide cycle. My advice is to plan launch and retrieve to coincide with the higher water periods from half flood to half ebb.

However, the approach to the boat ramp is very shallow and in dire need of dredging.

LAKERS CUTTING

The shell grit cutting at the bottom of Fellows Road, and Burnt Point (Melway refs 486 A10 to 486 D12), sometimes produces good size bream. Although they can be caught at various times throughout the year, the period around late August and early September, just as the water temperature begins to rise, is arguably the most productive time. They come right up into the pens above the road at times. At other times you have to do a bit of prospecting until you find them.

Quite a few bream are caught from Burnt Point itself (Melway ref 486 D12), which is accessible from the very end of McDonald Road, which in turn is a right angle extension of Fellows Road. From the end of McDonald Road you can walk in on a fairly defined track though the swamp, an exercise for which I suggest wearing waders or gum boots. The marine park boundary begins at the tip of Burnt Point but there is adequate signage to indicate just where this is.

LEFT: James Daglas with a nice bream from Lakers Cutting at Queenscliff.

BELOW: Jeff Richards with a nice snapper taken on the deep mud out from Indented Head.

CHAPTER 5
QUEENSCLIFF TO POINT LONSDALE

QUEENSCLIFF BOAT RAMP

There is presently a fee for 24 hour usage of the twin lane Queenscliff boat ramp which is located at the north east end of Hesse Street (Melway 487 A11). There is usually adequate parking here, except on public holidays in good weather. There are toilets and wash down facilities but no cleaning tables. The Queenscliff branch of the Australian Volunteer Coastguard is based here.

The ramp, which is sheltered in all but a strong northerly blow, gives access to both the sheltered waters within the Queenscliff boat harbour, Southern Port Phillip Bay and Port Phillip Heads approximately five kilometres to the South West.

QUEENSCLIFF BOAT HARBOUR

There is an extensive jetty complex and other structures within the harbour/marina (Melway ref 487 B11), some of which you may fish from, others not. The target species here is silver trevally. However, mullet, whiting and salmon are all caught here as well, along with the occasional good size pinkie snapper or tailor.

Gummy shark and good size snapper may also be present in this stretch of water from time to time but the large fleshy baits favoured for tempting these fish invariably attract large stingrays before anything else; making this type of fishing as difficult here as it is elsewhere.

QUEENSCLIFF PIER

The Queenscliff pier, on the main beach (Melway ref 487 A12), is all that remains of an extensive jetty complex dating back to the 1800s when

Queenscliff was a major fishing port producing mainly crayfish and barracouta. Barracouta no longer seem to be able to hold market share and crayfish populations have declined sharply from the days of my childhood when crayfish pots were often tied up along the pier.

As a teenager, I often rode my pushbike from North Geelong to Queenscliff and back on weekends to fish for leatherjacket down by the piles of the pier. When I'd caught enough that I could comfortably carry either in a bag across my handlebars or back, I cycled home with my booty. Even with the increasing siltation around the pier, that option remains today but few take advantage.

Be early for a spot on the Queenscliff pier because it is very popular among squid fishing enthusiasts of an evening. However, there is usually a spot vacant on the end where you can fish with the expectation of catching a good size whiting or flathead. A long cast from here at daybreak will pit you in with a chance at picking up a snapper as well.

BELL REEF

Exposed on the lowest tides, Bell Reef is situated below the white lighthouse on Shortlands Bluff (Melway ref 500 K2). Road access is from the south west end of Hesse Street, past the Naval College and into the Rip View car park. From here there is a rough pedestrian track down to the beach below and to Bell Reef to the left which is marked with a truncated cone, and more recently, a red port side marker.

You will need to wade through the shallow rocky channel for

LEFT: Roger Lewry with a good
catch of whiting from Queenscliff.

the last few metres to the reef, even on the lowest tides, but this is
not a problem with the appropriate clothing and footwear.

A variety of fish have been caught from Bell Reef over the years
including silver trevally, snapper and yellowtail kingfish. However,
in recent years Bell Reef has largely been taken over by squid fishing
enthusiasts. You may still catch snapper and sometimes silver
trevally here by casting out from the beacon end of the reef into
five to 10 m of water, depending on your casting ability. Naturally
enough, freshly caught squid is the most productive bait here.

In the past, casting suitable high density metal lures in the 40 to
100 gram range (depending on your tackle), along with the ability
to initiate a fast retrieve, has produced good catches of salmon from
Bell Reef along with occasional hook-ups on yellowtail kingfish,
and – with signs that the kingfish are returning – prospects for this
exercise have been encouraging.

PORT PHILLIP HEADS

Port Phillip Heads, both on the Queenscliff side and across at Point
Nepean, provides good fishing for whiting, salmon, snook, squid,

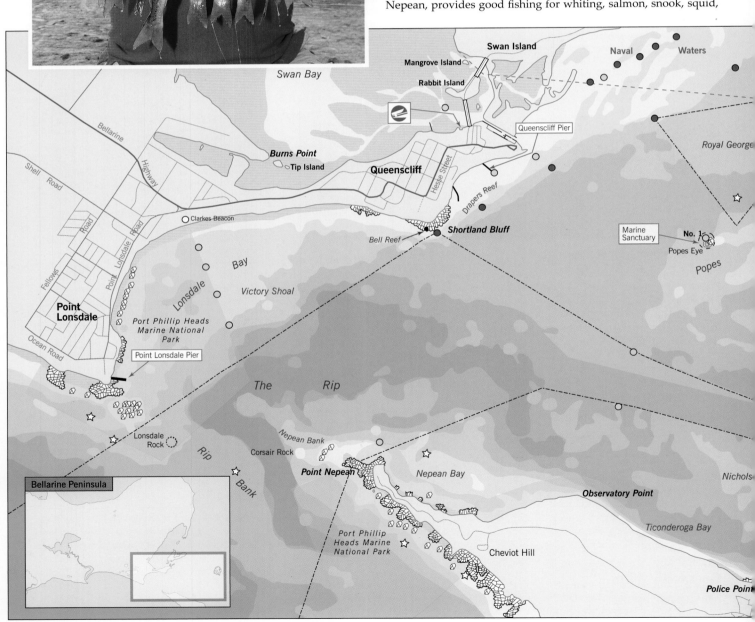

and – should you have the experience to handle the deeper water, which is severely tidal – large yellowtail kingfish as well.

Bluefin tuna also make an occasional appearance out here but the tuna, once common, have become rare to almost non-existent since the early 1980s due to increased, and ever more industrialised commercial fish harvesting on the high seas. Only recently have they shown signs of recovery as witnessed at Cape Otway and Portland in Western Victoria so we live in hope of their return to Port Phillip Heads.

TIDES AT PORT PHILLIP HEADS

It is important to note that the time of high and low tide at Port Phillip Heads refers only to the time at which the maximum and minimum water levels occur, not to the periods of slack water which occur approximately mid tide.

While this may be confusing, it is easily explained by the delay in the time it takes for either the rising or falling tide outside the Heads to reach equilibrium (slack water) with the water level, rising or falling, inside Port Phillip Bay.

ABOVE: David James with a colourful leatherjacket taken off Port Phillip Heads.

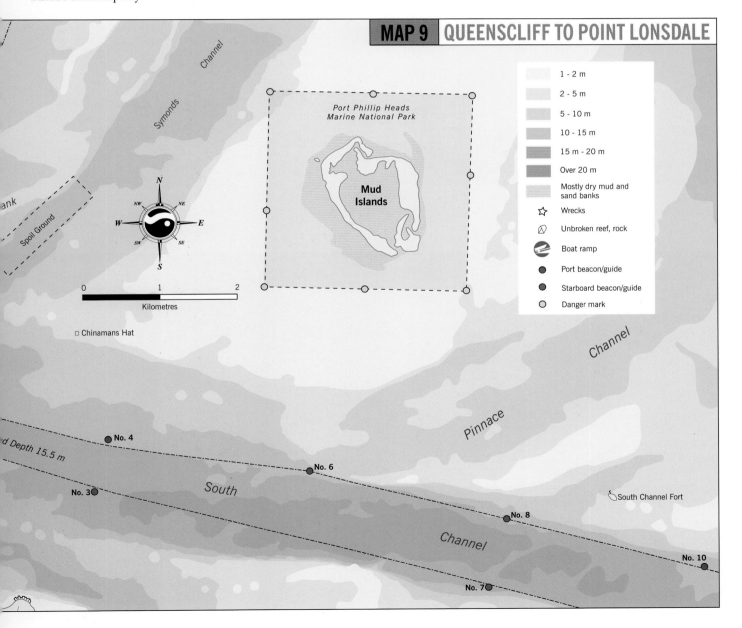

MAP 9 QUEENSCLIFF TO POINT LONSDALE

Port Phillip Heads
Marine National Park

Mud Islands

	1 - 2 m
	2 - 5 m
	5 - 10 m
	10 - 15 m
	15 m - 20 m
	Over 20 m
	Mostly dry mud and sand banks
☆	Wrecks
	Unbroken reef, rock
	Boat ramp
●	Port beacon/guide
●	Starboard beacon/guide
○	Danger mark

Channel

Symonds Channel

Spoil Ground

ank

N
NW NE
W E
SW SE
S

0   1   2
Kilometres

□ Chinamans Hat

Pinnace Channel

d Depth 15.5 m

No. 4

No. 6

No. 3

South

South Channel Fort

No. 8

Channel

No. 10

No. 7

SWAN ISLAND

There is an army base on Swan Island and you are not allowed to land here or enter the marked area defined by unsightly buoyage around its eastern and northern perimeters. However, there is good fishing for several species outside the prohibited area.

Whiting and squid are the main species caught along here with most of the good ground located to the south east of the water tower over the lifesavers boat shed on the Queenscliff Pier, out to the Coles Beacon which is locally known as the White Lady.

Snook (locally referred to as pike) may be taken whilst trolling the grass beds outside the buoyed perimeter with leaded handlines (leadlines), usually baited with a pilchard or garfish on a flight of ganged hooks, but lures may be used as well. Spring is the time for this exercise with October probably the most productive month.

Silver trevally may be taken at the wreck of the old J class submarine here but with some of the buoyage being moved further out, part of this wreck now lies within the prohibited area. While they are present in varying numbers throughout the years, September is probably the most productive month.

THE RIP

Fishing in The Rip is hazardous, especially if the ebb, or out flowing tide is confronting a southerly wind or swell. Additional hazards include large ships passing through Port Phillip Heads therefore the boat operator does need to be vigilant. This is in fact a seriously hazardous piece of water for the unwary.

Lining up the two lighthouses, the black over the white, gives a basic northeast/south west alignment, and as the piles on the Point Lonsdale Pier open to the west as you approach the Heads on that alignment during the ebb tide, you will reach the first patch of turbulent water; a potentially productive area for kingfish and Australian salmon. Whirlpools that noticeably affect the passage of small craft exist here but pose little risk to an experienced operator.

Progressing further out still, and especially should the outgoing tide be confronting a southerly wind or swell, the limits of small craft are clearly defined by row upon row of large pressure waves capable of capsizing a small craft or causing it to founder. You just have to watch the progress of large ships going through The Rip at such times to see how threatening these conditions can be.

SYMONDS CHANNEL

Gummy shark are present in all of the channels striating the area known as the Great Sand, erected on which are manmade features including Popes Eye, and South Channel Fort. Mud Island is also a conspicuous landmark between the Symonds and Pinnace channels but is a protected marine sanctuary for seagulls where you are not allowed to fish.

Travelling east at approximately 110 degrees from the Queenscliff harbour entrance you will reach the Symonds Channel after about 7.5 km (WGS84 ref 144 43 050 E x 38 16 720 S).

Symonds Channel does produce large gummy shark,

ABOVE: A butterfly gurnard taken at Port Phillip Heads.

BELOW: Danny Skene with a big gummy shark from the Symonds Channel off Queenscliff.

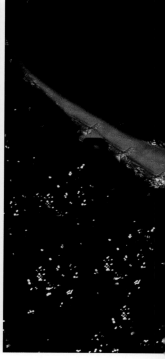

particularly at night, with the most favourable conditions being the tide coming in on evening with a south westerly breeze. However, the large and fleshy baits required for gummy shark do attract rays and sometimes, large sharks like the bronze whaler. Freshwater eel is preferred bait for large gummy shark because it outlasts other baits when under attack by pickers and the gummies love it.

Snapper are also an occasional catch in the Symonds Channel.

SNAPPER MARKS

Snapper are mainly taken on the drift at Port Phillip Heads because of anchoring restrictions imposed under Port Rule 62A. However, one of the few productive places you can fish at anchor for snapper with good expectations is between Bell Reef and the ground immediately in front of the black lighthouse.

Anglers fishing from boats anchor up for snapper close to, and within the approximate alignment of the red port side marker on Bell Reef with the prominent triangular marker known as Clarks Beacon to the WSW. (Melway ref 499 F12 & WGS84 ref 38 16 500 E x 144 39 700 S). The outgoing tide is the most productive time to fish for snapper here; either day or night. However the slower (neap) tides occurring several days prior to either the full or new moon produce the easiest fishing conditions here.

It should also be noted that the red piles which mark the drop off into deeper water, beginning just out from the Pilots Jetty and continuing north from the Queenscliff Harbour and Swan Island, offer snapper fishing potential. The outgoing tide along this drop off is the most productive time to fish for snapper here, once again though with the slower tides being favoured.

WHITING MARKS.

Whiting are the most commonly sought after fish at Queenscliff. They are caught in different areas, but suggestions of where to begin looking begin just south of the red pile in about 10 m of water about 400 m out from the Queenscliff harbour entrance (WGS84 ref 144 40 550 E x 38 16 080 S). This patch fishes best on the ebb tide.

The grass beds off Swan Island are also productive with most of the good fishing located south east of an alignment of the water tower over the lifeboat shed on the Queenscliff Pier.

Coles beacon, which is known locally as the 'white lady' sits almost directly off the northern and main entrance to Swan Bay and

marks the outer extremity of the recognized whiting ground off Swan Island (WGS84 ref 144 42 350 E x 38 14 300 S).

It should be noted that the deeper whiting marks, such as that off the harbour entrance and in the vicinity of Coles Beacon sometimes produce hook ups on snapper and gummy shark. Most are lost because of the difficulty in handling big fish in strong tides on light tackle.

SQUID

Squid may be caught almost anywhere off Queenscliff, but the incoming tide is best and by selecting a drift that will take you between the Pilots Jetty and the outer most red pile, you will cover productive ground, particularly as the incoming tidal current begins to ease toward slack water. However, beware the high point on Drapers Reef a little to the north east of the Pilots Jetty that has claimed many squid jigs over the years.

Lonsdale Bight is also worth a try for the larger squid which come in here to lay their eggs in late winter and spring but don't go into the marine park, the boundary of which is located below Clarks Beacon.

The grass beds off Swan Island to the north are also productive squid grounds and are easily accessible by turning left after leaving the harbour entrance. The squid here tend to be smaller than those taken south of the Queenscliff Jetty.

AUSTRALIAN SALMON

Salmon are present at Port Phillip Heads in good numbers from time to time, their presence being known by bird activity. Although present throughout the year, they tend to be both larger and more plentiful during the colder months of the year. Salmon may be taken on baits or lures; either cast out, or trolled behind the boat,

BELOW: Nazif Basic with two beautiful whiting taken from the Point Lonsdale Pier in Late June.

Another good size gummy shark comes alongside in the Symonds Channel off Queenscliff.

and sometimes by anglers casting lures from land based locations such as Bell Reef and the Point Lonsdale Pier.

Small rubber octopus imitations (rubber occy's) are a favoured lure for trolling; best rigged with a ball sinker, small enough to fit inside the body, with a straight hook like a Mustad Limerick 8260 or O'Shaughnessy 34007 patterns in size 3/0 or 4/0.

KINGFISH

Good size yellowtail kingfish have been scarce at Port Phillip Heads since the early nineties, but recent captures suggest they may be making a comeback.

Kingfish may be caught, both on handlines weighted at close intervals with barrel sinkers, and by surface trolling with gars, squid and lures that imitate them. The ebb tide is the most productive time to fish for kingfish in The Rip.

While kingfish have been caught at several locations at Port Phillip Heads, locations that have historically been productive, include:

THE WRECK

Inside The Heads, and over the wreck of the Eliza Ramsden (WGS84 ref 144 40 430 E x 38 17 680 S) has proven to be a productive kingfish ground for leadliners on the ebb tide, and at slack water, for those fishing more or less vertically with knife jigs and the like.

CHEVIOT HILL

Just inside Point Nepean there is a good place to anchor in 20 m or so during the ebb tide, allowing baits, or lures to work in the current with the expectation of a strike from a kingfish. Broadly, the area to fish for them may be located out from Cheviot Hill, (WGS84 ref 144 40 200 E x 38 17 800 S).

Anchor up here by high slack water, and should kingfish be present you may see them busting up on gars and squid at the surface as the tide begins running off. You may have to adjust your position to take advantage if they are appearing more or less constantly in the one spot, but don't go inside the Point Nepean marine park, the boundary of which is indicated by yellow buoys.

LONSDALE BIGHT

Be aware that the Point Lonsdale Marine Park begins in the Lonsdale Bight in front of Clarks Beacon, and when drift fishing on the ebb for whiting or squid you may have your number taken if you inadvertently drift into the Marine Park, so beware of that and ensure you keep outside the yellow markers.

The Bight does produce some really excellent whiting in the visible sand holes between the patches of reef although you rarely catch very many here, but those you do catch are invariably of good size. Like other areas that produce whiting, there is little point persisting in an area that's not producing any bites.

Much the same goes for squid, but should you be fortunate enough to spy a clutch of squid eggs on the bottom in the clear water you can rest assured there will be squid present in that spot and aggressively defending them.

GOLIGHTLY BEACH

(Melway 500 B2) This beach is located where the marine park begins so take care not to fish past the boundary which is adequately marked and situated beneath Clarks Beacon. With this in mind, you can fish this beach which is accessed from the shared pathway seaward of the skate park between the two roundabouts on Point Lonsdale Road. You can expect to catch good size whiting or pinkie snapper with a decent cast. Salmon may be taken here on bait and lures as well. Best results are to be had in the evenings and early mornings, particularly on the early flood tide.

Bill Athanasslies with a kingfish taken on a daisy chain of trolled garfish just outside Port Phillip Heads.

Sam Collins of Bendigo with a good size Kingfish taken at Port Phillip Heads.
(PHOTO COURTESY OF ADAMAS CHARTERS)

POINT LONSDALE OFFSHORE

Small kingfish may be present in good numbers just outside Port Phillip Heads. Beginning offshore from the Point Lonsdale back beach (WGS84 ref 144 34 500 E x 38 17 500 S) and zigzagging your way back toward the Point Lonsdale lighthouse, you can sometimes pick them up on your sounder. A leaded handline (lead line) baited with a strip of squid will usually take them if they are there. Keep outside the marine park though.

POINT LONSDALE PIER

Point Lonsdale pier (Melway ref 499 K6) is enormously popular, so much so it is often difficult to get a spot to fish day or night during holiday periods. Surf casting tackle is preferred by most who fish from the pier, but some just let their baits out under a float with the tide.

The incoming tide is the most productive and the easiest to fish with the current beginning to flow back in about three hours before the advertised time of high water at Port Phillip Heads.

Should there be sufficient space to do so safely, casting and retrieving suitable lures from the pier can be very productive on salmon as well, especially during the colder months of the year.

Although salmon are the main target species from the pier, silver trevally, snapper and good size King George whiting are always a chance too. Whiting are most common during the warmer months but may be present throughout the year.

Snapper tend to come on line from about the first week in September with the occasional good size fish being caught up until early December. March and April have been known to produce good size snapper from here as well.

Shark fishing enthusiasts use balloons or paravanes to send baits out on game fishing tackle from the pier to attract the attention of any good size sharks in the vicinity. Some beauties have been caught here, usually by anglers using generous portions of tuna. This bait has proven to be the most effective for this purpose time and again.

The target species here is the bronze whaler shark, which are a chance from November through until April with February the best month of all. However, the most commonly caught large shark from the pier is the ubiquitous seven-gilled shark which makes excellent flake but offers no challenge for the well-equipped angler.

LEFT: Alvin Josen with a catch of salmon from the Point Lonsdale Pier.

BELOW: Bill Athanasslies with a hefty bronze whaler taken from the Point Lonsdale Pier in March using a paravane to take his bait out.

CHAPTER 6
POINT LONSDALE TO JAN JUC

POINT LONSDALE TO BARWON HEADS

POINT LONSDALE OFFSHORE

As mentioned previously, small kingfish may be present in numbers just outside Port Phillip Heads which is within acceptable running time from Barwon Heads in good weather. Beginning offshore from the Point Lonsdale back beach (WGS84 ref 144 34 500 E x 38 17 500 S)

and zigzagging your way toward the Point Lonsdale lighthouse, you can sometimes pick them up on your sounder. Keep outside the marine park though.

Offshore from the Point Lonsdale back beach, more or less off the bottom of Fellows Road, there are some really good size whiting to be caught with fish over a kilogram not uncommon. You may

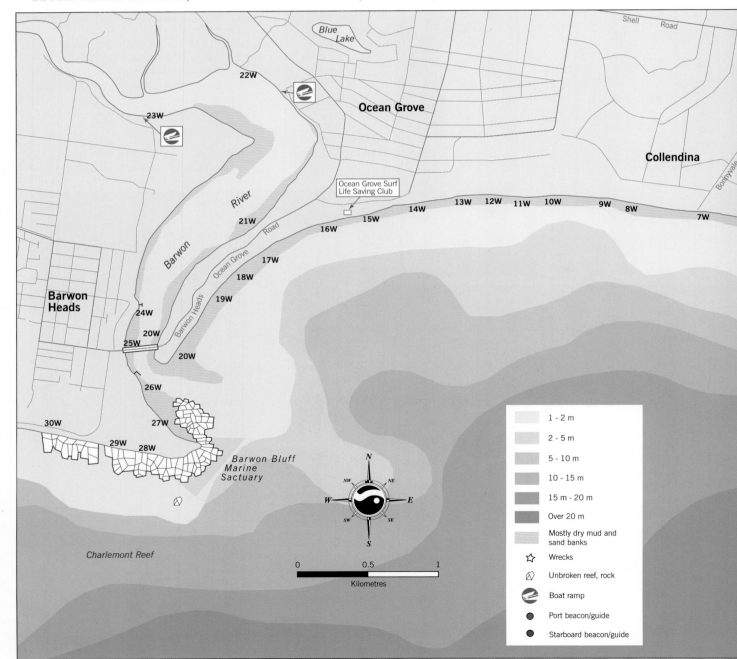

Blue Lake

Shell Road

22W

Ocean Grove

23W

Collendina

Bonnyvale

Ocean Grove Surf
Life Saving Club

River

14W 13W 12W 11W 10W 9W 8W 7W

21W   16W 15W

Barwon

Ocean Grove Road

17W

18W

Barwon Heads

19W

Barwon
Heads

24W

20W

25W

20W

26W

30W   27W

29W 28W

*Barwon Bluff
Marine
Sactuary*

Charlemont Reef

	1 - 2 m
	2 - 5 m
	5 - 10 m
	10 - 15 m
	15 m - 20 m
	Over 20 m
	Mostly dry mud and sand banks
☆	Wrecks
	Unbroken reef, rock
	Boat ramp
●	Port beacon/guide
●	Starboard beacon/guide

0   0.5   1
Kilometres

have to move a few times to find them, and although you may not catch many, we are talking class fish here.

OCEAN GROVE AND THIRTEENTH BEACH OFFSHORE

Boats launching from Barwon Heads have multiple options from pinkie snapper and whiting close inshore to larger snapper and gummy shark further out in around 40 m of water.

FORMBY AND CHARLEMONT REEFS

The reef complex known as the West Bank runs along the coast in front of the Barwon River mouth. High points include Formby Reef to the south east, just a few hundred metres past the wreck of the steamship SS Orungal, the boilers of which may be visible at low tide, and Charlemont Reef to the south west off Thirteenth Beach which breaks in all but the calmest seas.

The area around Formby Reef is noted for good catches of good size whiting and pinkie snapper. Charlemont Reef is hazardous in any significant swell and should be avoided in these conditions. Snook, pike and small kingfish have been caught in the vicinity of Charlemont Reef when sea conditions have been suitable.

THE FOUL GROUND

The offshore area known as the Foul Ground (WGS84 144 25 200 E x 38 20 300 S) has been a good starting point for a snapper drift with some good catches made out here. It is also a good area to anchor up and berley for school and gummy shark. However, you do need to be patient, sometimes berleying for several hours before the action goes down, usually in the early to mid afternoon.

Those familiar with the exit and entry to the Barwon estuary and who understand the limitations imposed by the tide cycle sometimes fish out here at night when the gummy shark taken after dark average a good deal larger than those taken during the day.

COLLENDINA AND OCEAN GROVE

The beach running to the west from the southern end of Fellows Road, Point Lonsdale (Melway ref 499 F6) to the Collendina Caravan Park, is inaccessible by road and with no beach access for vehicles, it is not really a proposition for most beach anglers. The beach itself is quite interesting though, interspersed with patches of reef, deep gutters and sand patches. This combination makes it ideal for whiting, pinkie snapper, salmon, and possibly many other species.

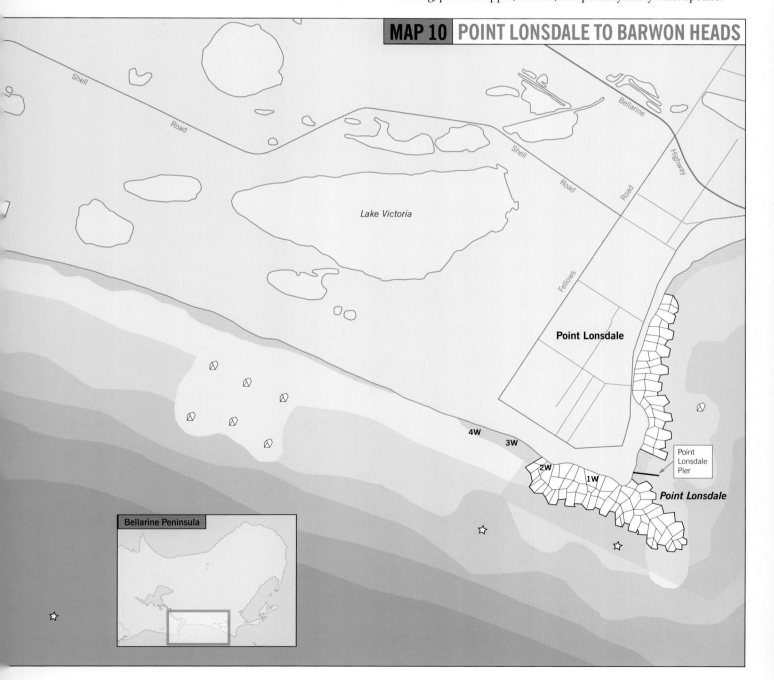

MAP 10 | **POINT LONSDALE TO BARWON HEADS**

Shell Road

Bellarine Highway

Shell Road

Lake Victoria

Fellows Road

Point Lonsdale

4W 3W

2W 1W

Point Lonsdale Pier

Point Lonsdale

Bellarine Peninsula

Travelling west from the bottom of Bonnyvale Road Collendina, the patches of reef thin out somewhat, stopping short of the Ocean Grove Lifesaving Club; area 15 W (Melway 497 G2).

Most of my fishing experience from this beach has been further toward the Barwon River mouth at areas 17, 18 and 19W where I have taken snapper and mulloway, along with various sharks and more skates and rays than I care to remember. Except for some isolated deeper holes, the beach becomes somewhat shallow at the base of the sand spit in front of 20W and I have not fished here. Never the less, snapper have been caught along here, mainly in the evening and after dark, during autumn and early winter.

While some anglers have been undeniably successful on the high tide along this beach catching mulloway and snapper, I have not. In my experience, the best time to fish these beaches has been when the tide is right out, allowing the angler to walk to the edge of the sand shelf and cast over the lip into what I would judge to be, about two metres of water. My suggestion is to cast well out with relatively small baits for snapper and in closer with larger baits when seeking mulloway,

On a suitably low tide in the evenings during the week immediately after a new or full moon in October, November or December, the beach will usually be uncovered, and in some cases, dry. In autumn though, the lowest tides occur early in the morning.

In winter, the evening tides do not always fall low enough to afford comfortable access. Never the less, this approach still works well here in winter although you may be standing in ankle deep water.

While others may have different approaches, mine has been to take a chair on which to hang my tackle and bait bags to keep them above the wet sand, and to use a good heavy rod spike to stand the rod in. Others, perhaps more dedicated than I, have used purpose-built structures, tripods and the like.

In my experience here, the best fishing occurs in the last hour of an ebb tide in the evening or early in the night, until the incoming tide forces you off the beach within about one and a half hours. My trips to the same areas on the morning low tides in autumn have not been productive, possibly because they were undertaken during daylight hours.

Neither Collendina nor Ocean Grove produce many salmon, which are the mainstay of surf anglers in Victoria and this has dissuaded many from fishing here. However, they do produce snapper, and the occasional mulloway to dedicated anglers prepared to invest the necessary time to have a realistic expectation of catching these prized species.

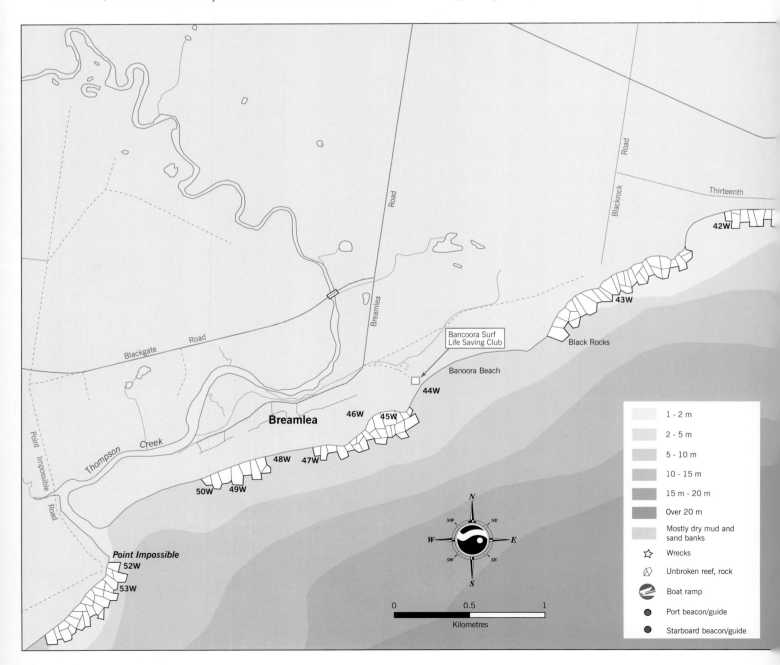

BARWON HEADS TO THOMPSON CREEK

THIRTEENTH BEACH

Thirteenth Beach begins in front of the Barwon Heads golf course to the west of the Barwon Heads Bluff and Barwon River Estuary. Access from Barwon Heads is via Ewing Blyth Drive, which becomes Thirteenth Beach Road and eventually meets Black Rock Road several kilometres to the west.

While Thirteenth Beach attracts mainly surfers, there are places to fish, particularly in the evening when most of the surfers have left. There is a good deal of reef interspersed at Thirteenth Beach resulting in gutters and holes supporting most coastal species of interest to anglers. Salmon are the main species here but large tailor have been caught by suitably prepared anglers, along with the occasional gummy shark, mulloway and snapper.

THE CYLINDERS

Following Ewing Blythe Drive, Barwon Heads, past The Bluff and around to the right at Thirteenth Beach, there are some good spots to fish the surf. The first spot is known as 'The Cylinders' at the eastern end of the beach at 31W. There is a sign indicating this beach and steps leading down. There is also a convenient parking area opposite.

There is a good deal of inshore reef here, and it is rather snaggy in places, but there is close access to deep water and the possibility of catching a variety of fish.

Another stretch of beach at the west end, between 40W (where there is a convenient parking area opposite the access track) and 42W. This section of beach is shallower than the former but worth fishing none the less.

BLACK ROCKS OUTFALL

The site of the old Black Rocks sewer outfall at the bottom of Black Rock Road (Melway 495 F5) is one of the few natural rock formations – albeit somewhat enhanced by previous public works – suitable to fish from along this part of the coast.

The main catch from here is pinkie snapper and good size whiting but at dawn and dusk there is always the chance of a good size snapper. It must be noted however, the ground is shallow and snaggy, accounting for many lost hooks and sinkers over the years.

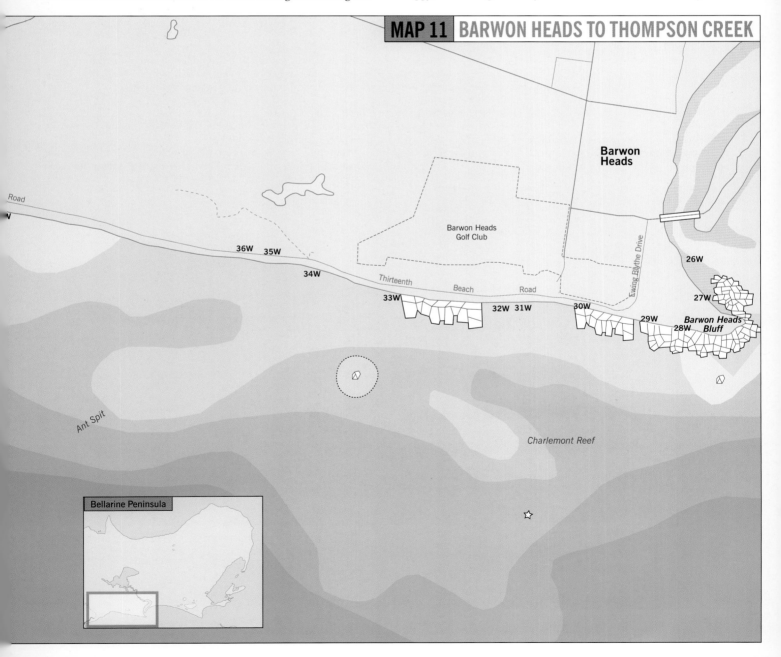

ABOVE: Chris Stamalos with a 20 kg school shark taken in 40 m of water offshore from Barwon Heads.

Some years ago, I investigated the possibility of this spot for seeking sharks land based. Using a balloon gas mixture in my balloons when the wind was from the northerly quarter and some ingenuity using a Lifesaver (candy with the hole) and a Big Splash Water Bomb to buoy the bait up to clear the shallow reef out in front – my contingent caught a total of six sharks (five bronze whalers and one thresher) in nine trips. For this reason I believe it is a proposition for suitably equipped anglers prepared to take advantage of winds blowing from the north.

BANCOORA BEACH

Bancoora Beach (Melway ref B, C & D 7) is accessed from the southern end of Bream Lea Road where you can park at the Bancoora Lifesaving Club. The beach lies between two sheltering reefs and is about 600 m in length with the deepest gutters beginning about halfway up the beach toward the eastern end. The beach terminates here against the western end of the "Black Rocks" reef complex known as 'The Wells'. The Wells refer to the natural springs in the vicinity; from which I once had to retrieve my pet dog at the time, Suzi that fell into one. Some of these wellsprings are quite deep and due to the vegetation they are not obvious, posing a risk to the unwary.

Bancoora Beach is the closest beach to Geelong. It is a good fishing beach with good low tide access to the sheltering reef on the right hand side from where you can catch salmon and other species. Mulloway have been taken here as well.

The west end of Bancoora Beach is a flagged area for swimmers but it does not seem to attract as many surfers as beaches at nearby Torquay and Jan Juc. The east end of the beach adjacent to The Wells is well worth trying on a high tide in the evening.

The rocks at the south west end of Bancoora Beach are accessible under suitable conditions of weather and tide, enabling the angler to cast, or float a bait out into the sheltered embayment formed by the reef. I have only caught salmon here whilst others have taken school mulloway in the evening after a very hot day.

BREAM LEA

Bream Lea is a small settlement on Thompson Creek at the bottom of Bream Lea Road (Melway 494 H8).

When the tide is in, you can usually catch mullet, small Australian salmon and one or two other species where the creek

ABOVE: Paul Harkins with a gummy shark taken aboard Adamas Charters off Barwon Heads.

LEFT: Mark Fowkes with an 8 kg snapper taken offshore from Barwon Heads.

ABOVE: Keith Fry, Craig Kitchen and Steve Avery with a sample of their school shark catch.

runs close in to the bank at the south west end of Horwood Drive. When the tide is out there is almost no water in this section of the creek and the only remaining water is on the other side of the exposed mud flats.

BUCKLEYS BAY

Buckleys Bay, the beach on the south side of Bream Lea, is accessible from several walking tracks but the streets from which these tracks lead are designated no parking areas, so you would have to park along Horwood Drive should you want to fish this beach, which receives little attention from anglers and surfers. The beach directly in front of Scott Street (50W & Melway ref 494 H9) is productive for salmon on a rising tide.

POINT IMPOSSIBLE

Point Impossible itself (Melway 494 F10), offers little in the way of fishing opportunities. I have drifted baits out from the creek mouth with the running out tide of an evening but caught nothing for my efforts. Point Impossible Road, which is accessible from Blackgate Road, gives access to the lower reach of Thompson Creek (Melway ref 494 F9). Here there is room to park your car off the narrow unmade road where you can catch Australian salmon and mullet when the tide is in and there is a good amount of water within the creek.

Over the years I have caught small but legal size Australian

salmon to use as live bait in the Barwon Estuary for mulloway. With the tide coming in toward full as the sun goes down; casting a small metal wobbler or spoon usually produces strike after strike. Unfortunately, the creek mouth sometimes closes and this entertaining, and very useful fishery, is temporarily lost.

THOMPSON CREEK UPPER ESTUARY

A local and alternative name for Thompson Creek is Bream Creek. However, the reach downstream from Blackgate Road (Melway 495 A6) is fairly shallow, and when the entrance is open; tidal and almost dry at low tide. I've not seen any bream taken here. Above Blackgate Road is another story. While there is a walk of several hundred metres before you reach the deeper, more productive pools and snaggy timber filled reaches where both bream and estuary perch call home, this water does not receive a lot of pressure from anglers. Unfortunately it is illegally netted from time to time so more angler presence would be beneficial.

Once you round the first bend upstream from the Blackgate Road Bridge, the estuary becomes more attractive to anglers and their quarry. Further upstream, access beyond what many would consider reasonable walking distance, is from Dans Reserve on McCanns Road (Melway 494 F1). There is limited bank access where you can fish and also launching facilities for a kayak or even small rowing boat but this is covered in greater detail in the chapter eight.

THOMPSON CREEK TO JAN JUC

TORQUAY BOAT RAMP

The twin concrete boat ramp at Torquay (Melway ref 506 B5) is located in front of the Torquay Angling Club in the beach reserve at the bottom of Beach Road after crossing The Esplanade. There is a launch fee payable to the honesty box at the club rooms.

Unlike the beautifully designed, slatted timber ramp it replaced,

the current ramp is virtually a concrete breakwater that traps sand; making the ramp all but useless for its intended purpose.

Never the less, anglers do launch their boats from here; locals sometimes using tractors or extended lengths of rope (sometimes 30 m or more) enabling boat trailers to be detached while boats are man-handled on and off trailers.

MAP 12 THOMPSON CREEK TO JAN JUC

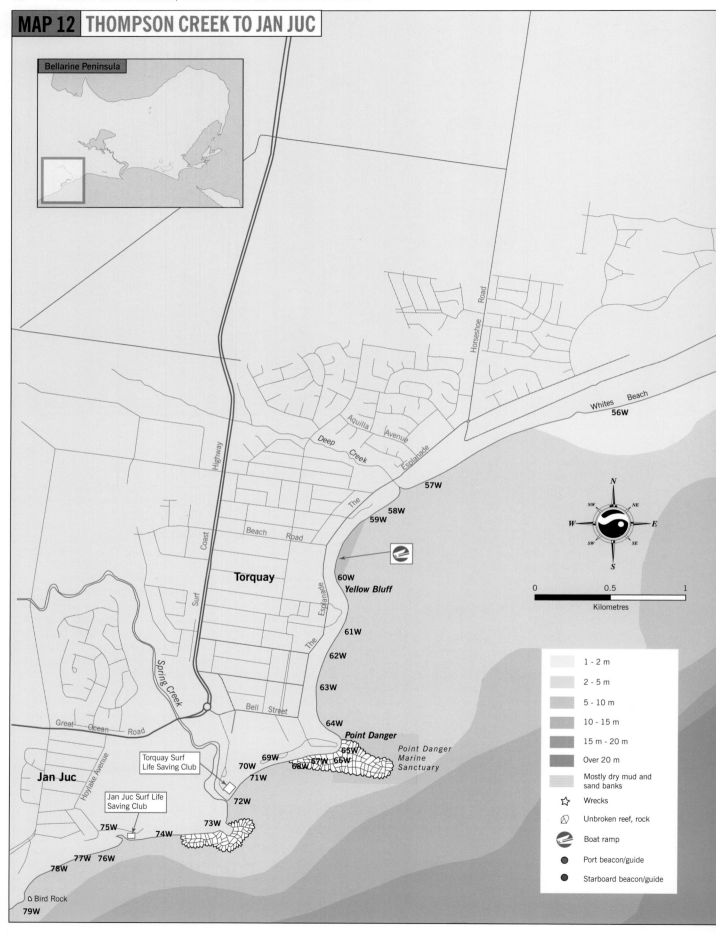

Bellarine Peninsula

Whites Beach
56W

Horseshoe Road

Aquilla Avenue

Deep Creek

The Esplanade

57W
58W
59W

60W
Yellow Bluff

The Esplanade

61W

62W

63W

64W

Beach Road

Coast Highway

Surf Coast Highway

Torquay

Spring Creek

Bell Street

Great Ocean Road

Point Danger

Point Danger
Marine
Sanctuary

65W
67W 66W
68W
69W
70W
71W
72W

Torquay Surf
Life Saving Club

Jan Juc Surf Life
Saving Club

Jan Juc

Hoylake Avenue

73W

75W
74W

77W 76W
78W

o Bird Rock
79W

N
NW NE
W E
SW SE
S

0   0.5   1
Kilometres

	1 - 2 m
	2 - 5 m
	5 - 10 m
	10 - 15 m
	15 m - 20 m
	Over 20 m
	Mostly dry mud and sand banks
☆	Wrecks
⬙	Unbroken reef, rock
⬀	Boat ramp
●	Port beacon/guide
●	Starboard beacon/guide

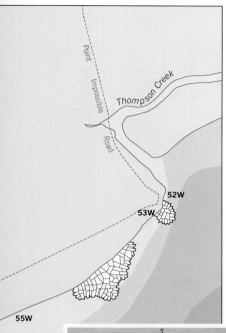

WHITES BEACH

Whites Beach (56W & Melway ref 506 G2) is accessed from The Esplanade north east of the Horseshoe Bend Road roundabout. It produces pinkie snapper and good size whiting on dusk with a low tide providing best access to the deepest water. The beach is interspersed with reef and quite snaggy but it is productive none the less.

DEEP CREEK BEACH

At the bottom of Aquilla Avenue (57W & Melway 506 C4) this beach affords the angler the similar prospects and challenges to Whites Beach. It's an area where I have caught good size whiting at daybreak.

FISHERMANS BEACH

Between the Torquay Motor Yacht and Angling Club (60W) and the Torquay Sailing Club (59W), Torquay's Fishermans Beach is not an especially renowned fishing spot and does not receive much attention from anglers. However, from late August till late September there are prospects of catching good size snapper from this beach especially on evening and after dark. Fishermens Beach north is a boating exclusion zone.

BOTTOM: Jamie Karamatic with a thresher shark taken off Torquay.

BELOW: Matt Grgic with a nice snapper taken offshore from Jan Juc

QUIET CORNER

Between Yellow Bluff and the marine park on Point Danger, Quiet Corner (Melway ref 506 B7&8) is a shallow beach where you can pump bass yabbies for bait when the tide falls low enough to expose their holes. Good size whiting may be caught from the beach at times, particularly toward evening. Quiet corner is a boating exclusion zone.

SPRING CREEK BEACH

Popular with surfers during the day, the beach at the mouth of Spring Creek (72W & Melway ref 505 K9) offers good prospects for salmon, along with the occasional snapper, gummy shark and mulloway for anglers fishing the evening and into the night.

SPRING CREEK

Spring Creek at Torquay (Melway ref 505 J7 – K9), although rarely fished except by a handful of knowledgeable anglers, contains a good population of bream, mullet and possibly estuary perch. Large sea mullet are also present. This body of water is usually land-locked and openings to the sea are usually rare and short lived events. There is ample parking alongside Spring Creek and there is a board walk giving access to both sides of the creek.

JAN JUC

The beach with the closest vehicle access at Jan Juc is alongside, and to the north of, the Jan Juc Surf Life Saving Club (74W & Melway ref 505 J10). Popular with surfers by day, the best fishing proposition is during a high tide on dusk or later into the night. Access is via Hoylake Avenue from the Great Ocean Road then down Surf Club Road where there are speed humps and a nominated speed limit of 10 km/h. Salmon are taken here on the high rising tide toward evening, and gummy shark are a good chance after dark.

At the opposite (south west) end of the beach (Melway 505 G11) adjacent to the reef that includes the notable Bird Rock, the beach formation is less attractive to surfers because the waves tend not to break very far off the beach. It's a productive spot to fish with a high tide in the late evening with salmon being the main catch and the chance of a gummy shark or mulloway after dark.

CHAPTER 7
THE BARWON ESTUARY

ABOVE: Jamie Behrens with a 52 cm estuary perch from the tributary opposite the Sheepwash Boat Ramp.

BOAT RAMPS

SHEEPWASH (PELICAN COURT) RAMP
The Sheepwash boat ramp (Melway 483 C11) is located by turning right at the bottom of Sheepwash Road into River Parade then looking for the fourth opening on the left opposite Pelican Court. The Sheepwash boat ramp is a modest affair but drops away into at least two metres of water on the lowest tides, enabling even large trailer boats to be launched here. There is a small mooring pontoon and adequate parking except for public holidays in daylight hours during good weather.

MINAH STREET RAMP
There is another small, single-lane ramp suitable for small craft in front of Minah Street (Melway ref 483 B11). This modest structure becomes unusable at low tide so calculations need to be made.

OCEAN GROVE
Coming from the Bellarine Highway, the Ocean Grove boat ramp (Melway 483 E11) is reached via Guthridge Street from Wallington Road (the first turn right after descending the steep hill into Ocean Grove). Turn right through the car park in front of the Ocean Grove Golf Course to reach the boat ramp and pontoons at the far end. The ramp is suitable for large trailer boats with at least two metres of water on the very lowest tides. There are two large mooring pontoons and usually adequate vehicle and trailer parking.

ACCESS
The Barwon estuary is permanently open to the sea but the estuary between the boat ramps and the sea is shallow with no defined channel and hazardous at low tide with a good deal of reef that has regularly damaged boat propellers. My advice is to time both your exit from and re-entry to the river between half flood to half ebb to lessen the chance of hitting the bottom which is not far beneath the surface in low water conditions.

The low tides in the evenings from September to December can be particularly low and hazardous. My advice is to not plan trips that involve re-entry to the estuary at these times. The early morning low tides in autumn and early winter are similarly problematic, but there is almost no boat traffic at these times.

SPECIES
Species present is the lower Barwon estuary throughout the year that are readily caught by the casual angler, include Australian salmon (usually small), mullet, King George whiting and silver trevally along with a variety of rays and sometimes small sharks. Other species that may be present from time to time include snapper, elephant fish, cowanyoung and mulloway.

DOWNSTREAM STRUCTURES
The most productive time to begin fishing the downstream structures at Barwon Heads, which include the bridge, the Ozone

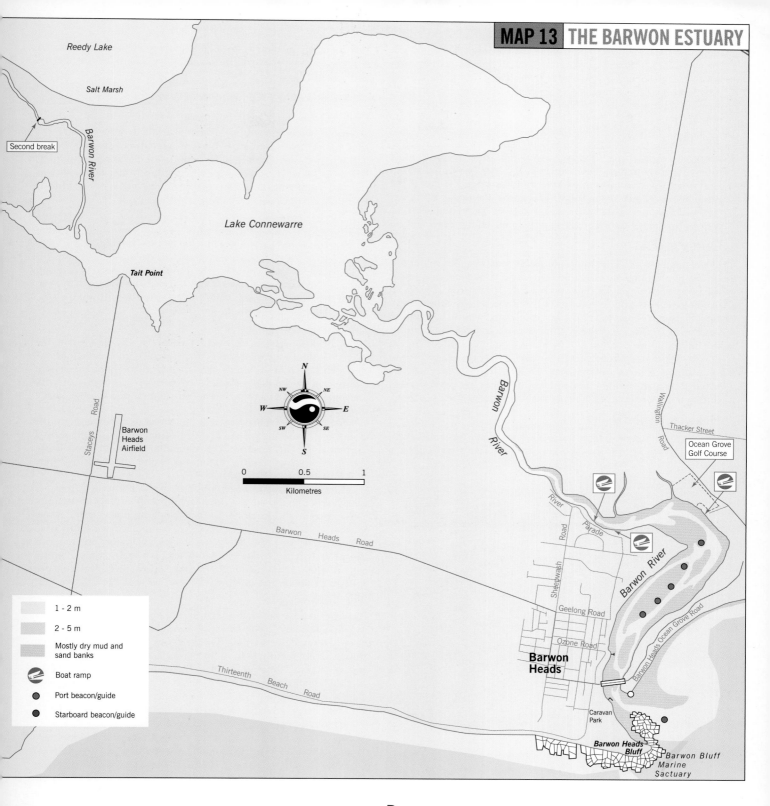

MAP 13 THE BARWON ESTUARY

Reedy Lake

Salt Marsh

Second break

Barwon River

Lake Connewarre

Tait Point

Staceys Road

Barwon Heads Airfield

N
NW *NE*
W *E*
SW *SE*
S

0   0.5   1
Kilometres

Barwon River

Wallington Road

Thacker Street

Ocean Grove Golf Course

Barwon Heads Road

River Road

Parade

Sheepwash Road

Geelong Road

Ozone Road

Barwon River

Barwon Heads Ocean Grove Road

Barwon Heads

Thirteenth Beach Road

Caravan Park

Barwon Heads Bluff

Barwon Bluff Marine Sactuary

1 - 2 m

2 - 5 m

Mostly dry mud and sand banks

Boat ramp

Port beacon/guide

Starboard beacon/guide

Road Jetty upstream, and the Fishermen's Jetty downstream (Melway 497 C4 & 5), is during the first two hours of the incoming tide.

To calculate the start of the incoming tide in the lower estuary is to add two hours to the advertised time of low water at Port Phillip Heads. This will give you the time of slack water in the lower estuary. Should there be any significant increase flow from the Barwon upstream, slack water may be delayed for another hour; so be patient.

Looking up the tide times for Barwon Heads gives only high and low water and not high or low slack water, which is the information required by anglers.

DOWNSTREAM TO THE MOUTH

Downstream from the bridge on the Ocean Grove side of the river, the sand spit provides land based access to productive water on the very last of the ebb and early flood. Following low slack water, there is little current here, making this expanse of sand a good angling option for species such as mullet, Australian salmon and silver trevally. This situation remains, unless the rising tide advances to the point where the angler has to retreat, which would only be the case on the highest tides.

Directly downstream from the Fishermen's Jetty on the Barwon Heads side of the river, a channel of variable depth runs right alongside the bank directly in front of the Foreshore Caravan Park for about 200 m before crossing to the white flashing navigation light on the opposite side of the river. There are good fishing prospects here for a number of species. For reasons relating to access and productivity, this area should be fished on the last of the ebb tide and the first of the flood.

THE FALLS

After crossing back to the Ocean Grove side of the river, the channel briefly narrows to just a few metres as it passes through a gap in heavy reef. The channel is marked by a white navigation light to the north and a red pile to the south. This gap in the reef is known as 'The Falls' because of the disparate water levels above and below as the reef becomes exposed on the most extreme falling tides.

OUTER REACH

Downstream from The Falls, the outer reach of the estuary is productive ground but only for experienced anglers who know the geographical peculiarities and hazards of this area. Here of an evening, when the tide is running out, really good size King George whiting, snapper and the occasional mulloway have all been taken. Anchoring in this lower reach of the Barwon Estuary is unsafe on the incoming tide because of dangerous incoming swells. Whiting may be taken here, in respect to the tide sequence, at any time of year although their numbers are variable. Snapper may also be taken from April until at least June. Mulloway are often present during the last couple of hours of the ebb or run-off tide.

BARWON HEADS BLUFF

You may no longer fish from the rocks below and to the right of the Barwon Heads Bluff (Melway 497 D6) because it has been declared a

marine park. The bluff is still a good place to view the river mouth and to get a perspective on reef contours, sand bars and the like; it's well worth a look.

UPSTREAM FEATURES AND STRUCTURES

OCEAN GROVE BOAT RAMP PONTOONS

There are two pontoons, one upstream and one downstream from the Ocean Grove boat ramp in front of the Ocean Grove golf course. The pontoons are specifically for boats using the ramp as opposed to fishing; however, there is a good depth of water here and you may fish from these structures provided you retrieve your lines at the approach of vessels preparing to pull alongside.

THE BLIND CHANNEL

The broad shallow sand and mud promontory featuring some mangroves on the Barwon Heads side of the river (Melway ref 483 D,E 12) is bisected by a narrow gutter known as the Blind Channel. It is partially navigable by small boat only. Its entrance is between port side (red) channel markers 8 and 10 and runs to the north west. It is a very small body of water but has produced silver trevally, cowanyoung, mullet and salmon.

THE SHEEPWASH

From the Sheepwash boat ramp at Barwon Heads, upstream to the reserve at the west end of River Parade, there is good vehicle access and you can drive to where you want to fish. There are several purpose-built wooden structures from where you can fish with the expectation of catching the most common species that I have already mentioned.

Fishing times here are not as critical as they are in the downstream section but the first two hours of the incoming tidal current is still the most productive time to fish. In the Sheepwash, the low tide change is three to four hours after the advertised time of low water at Port Phillip Heads.

Additional species to be taken from the Sheepwash that are rarely encountered in the downstream sections include estuary perch, bream and luderick. Estuary perch are most active in the warmer months of the year and have been taken within the two tributaries on the north side of the Sheepwash. Bream and luderick are present both in the tributaries and the main stream during winter where I have caught them either side of high slack water in the late afternoon and evening.

THE TRIBUTARIES

Two tributaries exist on the north side of the Sheepwash and access is principally by kayak or dinghy. Although they are relatively deep, averaging better than two metres in the lower reaches; both entrances are separated from the main stream by shallow entrance bars and inaccessible but for the shallowest craft except at high tide.

The downstream tributary marks the western boundary of the Ocean Grove golf course, the entrance being only a couple of hundred metres from the Ocean Grove boat ramp (Melway ref 483 E10). Land based access from here is marginal because of the soft, muddy ground. There is also marginal land based access to this tributary from Wallington Road where you can walk in (with gumboots) from the bus stop opposite the bottom or west end of Thacker Street Ocean Grove (Melway ref 483 D8). This tributary, although barely navigable in the mid section, rejoins the main stream between the Sheepwash and Lake Connewarre.

The entrance to the upstream tributary (Melway ref 483 C11) is virtually opposite the Sheepwash boat ramp. With a shallow bar across the entrance, it's only accessible by kayak or dinghy and eventually becomes shallow, narrow and ultimately reaches a dead end in the Wallington wetlands. Never the less it offers excellent potential for light tackle enthusiasts in kayaks seeking the species specifically referred to.

There are other small tributaries upstream from the Sheepwash that I have not investigated, but like the two I've already mentioned, they drain the extensive, low-lying Wallington wetlands.

ABOVE: Daniel and Jayden Werner with a good sample of silver trevally and salmon from the Barwon Estuary near the Ocean Grove Ramp.

LEFT: Robert Coon with a 4.5 kg snapper from the Barwon estuary on the April full moon.

BELOW: Kassidy and Jayden Werner with a sample of their catch of bream and mullet from the Barwon Estuary

THE THUNDERBOLT

The Thunderbolt is a long standing local name for the winding section of estuary between Lake Connewarre and the Sheepwash.

Upstream access to the Barwon above the Sheepwash is limited. Gone are the days you could drive in from Lake Road, Connewarre, at the risk of getting bogged I might say, and fish the area known as the Thunderbolt. You can still fish this upstream section from a boat; however, the upstream section below Lake Connewarre has become rather shallow over past decades and access to the lake from the river is now problematic and seems to be growing more so every year.

You can walk in a certain distance from River Parade West, which is accessible by turning left at the bottom of Sheepwash Road until you come to the reserve where you can park your vehicle. The first promontory (Melway ref 483 A10) is not far, it's what we used to call the first fence. On the incoming tide an eddy forms behind the point which makes it ideal for fishing at this time.

The next suitable point to fish from is a good deal further and obstructed by a couple of small drains or channels which I could easily jump over in my youth, alas not now. The point is a little further on after the second fence and the vegetation on this point is noticeably greener than most of the vegetation along the river bank. This point also initiates an eddy on the incoming tide and is an excellent spot from which to fish on the incoming tide.

Walking in further than this becomes problematic because the ground is soft and muddy with small drains that need to be negotiated, never the less some folk do and are, hopefully, rewarded for their efforts.

LAKE CONNEWARRE

Lake Connewarre is shallow and is becoming more so, never the less it does support good populations of most of the fish found elsewhere in the system. During the sixties, und undoubtedly much earlier, it was netted illegally and regularly. The recent popularity of this body of water with kayakers and people in general has hopefully minimised illegal commercial fish harvesting here.

SECOND BREAK

The Second Break (Melway 467 E11) divides the estuarine section of the Barwon, including Lake Connewarre, from the fresh water section above.

The stretch of river between the second break and Lake Connewarre produces some beautiful bream, as well as estuary perch for those who know how to catch them. Most of the other species found in the Barwon Estuary, including mulloway, may be found in this section of the river from time to time but the target species here are estuary perch and bream. Having said this, large brown trout are sometimes present in the pool directly below the Second Break where they have been caught over several decades by the handful of dedicated anglers who seek them. Sometimes present in Lake Connewarre as well, they do not seem to be present in the lower reaches of the estuary as would be the case if they were sea-run fish. I would suggest they've most likely come over the break during high water levels along with the ubiquitous European carp that ultimately die in the brackish water, sometimes in large numbers, making quite a stench.

TAIT POINT

Tait Point is accessible by turning north into Stacey's Road from the Barwon Heads Road at the Barwon Heads Airport (Melway ref 481 G10). You can fish from Tait Point and although the water is not very deep here, there are bream and mullet to be caught at times, along with eels after dark.

Access to the upper Barwon Estuary below the second break is by kayak or small dinghy from the Tait Point boat ramp (Melway 481 H4).

After launching at Tait Point, the river mouth may be reached by taking the West Arm of the lake. This involves following the bank around to the left after launching before proceeding for about 500 m up the west arm until you reach the second opening in the reeds on the right hand side.

The entrance is discreet and may not be obvious but this is the Barwon River. There is a shallow bar across the entrance that may require the occupants of even small craft to push across with an oar or paddle until inside the river which is about 2.5 to 3 m deep for most of the way up to the weir known as the Second Break, a distance I would judge to be about a kilometre.

CHAPTER 8
FRESHWATER FISHING AROUND GEELONG

ABOVE: There is kayak access to Thompson Creek at Dans Reserve off McCanns Road.

BARWON RIVER

The Barwon River runs right through Geelong and is fresh downstream to the weir known as the Second Break; a distance of approximately eight kilometres from Geelong by water.

BREAKWATER

The Barwon River at Breakwater (Melway 466 C1) is popular with anglers who mainly catch carp and redfin, along with the occasional tench or brown trout. Eels are also present and are caught mainly at night. Large brown trout are sometimes sighted in this section of river but rarely caught. Access is available from Breakwater Road beneath the Railway Bridge where you can park your car near the bank of the river on either side. This may not be a permanent situation though because of ongoing major road works.

Upstream, the river follows the Belmont golf course to the Moorabool Street Bridge but access is by bicycle and walking path only.

BOAT RAMP

There is a ramp on the Barwon just downstream from the Moorabool Street Bridge (Melway ref 452 A8) for which a permit is required from the Corangamite Catchment Authority 5232 9100. Although you may fish from the bank, you are not permitted to fish from a boat between the Ford at Breakwater and the Shannon Avenue Bridge as this area is reserved for rowing and water skiing. Above the Shannon Avenue Bridge (451 E9) you may fish from an unpowered craft like a rowing boat or kayak.

QUEENS PARK AND BUCKLEY FALLS

Coming down Aphrasia Street Newtown/Queens Park Road, you may access the river from a small car park adjacent to the river on the left hand side after crossing the single lane Queens Park Bridge (Melway ref 451 D4). There is good bank access here from which you can catch carp, redfin, tench and eels. Brown trout may also be caught here on occasion. There is additional access a little further along, north of Queens Park Road and further along still, on the right had side of the road. Going up the hill is the road leading into the Buckley Falls Reserve (Melway ref. 451 B4).

The Barwon River at Queens Park and Buckley Falls (Melway ref 451 and 450 K4), regularly produces brown trout on both bait and lures, particularly during winter but before the water becomes high and discoloured from annual rains.

Good catches of redfin have been made on lures downstream from Buckley Falls and around the Queens Park golf course, particularly by anglers covering some ground while casting lures. Tench to almost three kilograms have been taken by dedicated coarse fishermen in this section of the river, but they prove elusive to most anglers.

The large pool directly below Buckley Falls contains a variety of freshwater fish. Those of interest to anglers include redfin, brown trout and tench. There are eels as well for those prepared to fish into the night. Native grayling are also present but rarely become obvious except for warm summer evenings when they feed towards the surface on small insects.

Seagull Paddock

The Cowies Creek lagoon, where it runs through the Seagull Paddock Reserve in Norlane (Melway 441 K3) is regularly stocked with yearling rainbow trout prior to school holidays to allow youngsters to try their luck. Vehicle access is from Birdwood Avenue off The Boulevard and by shared trail from the north end of Edols Street, North Geelong.

St Augustines Waterhole

This small body of water adjacent to the roundabout on South Valley Road Highton (Melway 451 B4) is also regularly stocked with yearling rainbow trout prior to school holidays to allow youngsters to try their luck.

McLeods Waterhole

McLeods Waterholes on Wyndham Street running off the east side of Jetty Road, Clifton Springs (Melway 456 G10) and Lake Lorne near the old Drysdale railway station (Melway 456 F12) contain a variety of fish including golden perch and roach. Shrimp may be collected with a dip net against bankside foliage. Unfortunately, European carp dominate angler's catches from these waters during the day, and eels come on the bite after dark.

Thompson Creek

Access to the freshwater section of Thompson Creek is from Horseshoe Bend Road (Melway 493 K1) and from Dans Reserve on McCanns Road (Melway 494 F1). There is a launching point for kayaks on Dans Reserve.

Although it is a small creek, it does possess a number of deep holes containing good size redfin that can be caught on lures by anglers with the skills to fish discreet locations such as this.

Lake Modewarre

Lake Modewarre (Melway X911 C8), is a small lake, just over 400 hectares. It is approximately 25 km from Geelong, just off the Princes

ABOVE: Chris Stamalos and Andrew Phillips with their catch of tench, brown trout and redfin from Wurdi Boluc Reservoir.

RIGHT: Jim Robinson with a nice brown trout from the Barwon above Ceres.

Highway on Waltons Road. It has a boat ramp and reasonable bank access. At the time of writing, Lake Modewarre is still recovering from the dry spell ending in 2010/11 and is yet to be stocked. With the continuance of seasonal rains there is no doubt this water will again be stocked with brown and rainbow trout and again be the waterway that it once was.

Lake Murdeduke

Lake Murdeduke (Melway A7) covers approximately 1,100 hectares near Winchelsea, about 40 km from Geelong on the Princes Highway. Turn off to the lake via Gosney Street which leads to a fork in the road just before the lake.

The right fork leads to Shelford with access to the lake from Block Lane on the left. The left fork goes to Cressy and provides access to the lake from the road causeway and through the Department of Conservation and Natural Resources reserve on the right having crossed the causeway. Lake Murdeduke once had a reputation as a world class rainbow trout fishery. Sadly, management of this fishery, even at its peak was minimal; the lake has practically no amenities, as well as a substandard boat ramp.

Wurdi Boluc Reservoir

Wurdi Boluc reservoir (Melway ref X911 B/C 8/9) is located about 30 km from Geelong on the Cape Otway Road and covers about 400 hectares. There is a parking area with a sign showing the areas where anglers may fish. Wurdi Boluc Reservoir is a domestic water supply and boating is not permitted. This water contains rainbow and brown trout as well as redfin, roach and eels, all of which grow comparatively large in this water. Golden perch have reportedly been taken from here as well. There are gudgeon and minnow present and these are frequently captured and used as bait by anglers.

The Moorabool River

The Moorabool joins the Barwon at Queens Park (Melway 451 B3). The lower Moorabool River was once a magnificent scenic stream skirting the outskirts of Geelong, producing brown and rainbow trout, redfin and the occasional good size native blackfish. The heartbreaking aspect of this section of the Moorabool River is its deterioration from the wonderful prolific stream that it was when friends and I accessed it from the western end of Church Street, Hamlyn Heights, by pushbike back in the late 1950s to the drain it has now become.

I've heard there are plans to increase so-called environmental flows to the river but the health of the lower Moorabool and its fisheries are dependent on water being released from Lal Lal Reservoir. In recent times at least, that release of water has been insufficient. However, with the easing of drought conditions at the time of putting together this publication, some improvement in the lower Moorabool may be expected.

Upper Moorabool River

The Moorabool River has its twin origins on the southern slopes of the Great Dividing Range north west of Ballan. Five reservoirs are located on its east and west branches, three of which are open to fishing. Although in excess of an hour's travelling time from Geelong, these reservoirs remain popular and productive fishing destinations. Of course there are many places other than the reservoirs where you could fish along both branches of the upper Moorabool River, some obvious, some discreet, but much of these places lie on private property where you would be required to ask permission for access. For for the purpose of this publication, I will concentrate on the reservoirs, which receive most attention from anglers who fish from the bank. Fishing from boats, or from man-made structures on these waters is not permitted.

The East Branch

On the east branch of Moorabool River, travelling from north to south, there is Korweinguboora, which is a small local water supply

ABOVE: Phil Walker with a 4.55 kg brown that he caught on a Jackal TN60 from Wurdi Boluc Reservoir.

that is closed to fishing. Bolwarrah (Hunts) Reservoir (7.5 hectares) is accessible from the Daylesford-Ballan Road, then Dehnerts Road from Bunding and Bostock Reservoir (about 100 hectares) which is the most popular with anglers and accessible by taking the Ballan exit from the Western Freeway are both open to fishing in respect of current regulations.

The West Branch

On the west branch of the Moorabool River, travelling from north to south is the Moorabool Reservoir (about 160 hectares). Historically, it has contained brown trout, both from departmental stocking and allegedly from the Moorabool River's small but self-sustaining populations. This water also contains redfin and tench. Access to Moorabool Reservoir is from Spargo Creek Road, Bolwarrah, or from Springbank via Ormond Road then Linehans Road.

Although still listed as angling water on the Department of Primary Industries Website, access to the Moorabool Reservoir was closed at the Central Highlands Water Board during the drought that began in the late nineties and continued till 2010. At the time of writing, this reservoir is fenced off with locked gates on every access point displaying deterrent signage. Unfortunately, access to this water, which has been open to fishing from 1924, and has been the venue of national fishing competitions is currently under review and hopefully soon to be restored.

Lal Lal Reservoir

Unfortunately Lal Lal Reservoir, also known as Bungal Dam is closed to fishing except for special events that in the past have been run through the Geelong and District Association of Angling Clubs in association with Geelong and District Water Board (now replaced by Barwon Water). Unfortunately, those trips seem to have disappeared with the extended drought. Never the less, this water has been home to a thriving population of brown trout and that may still be the case.